What people are say

Fairy Que

Morgan has created a guide filled with practical and personal insights to help both the curious scholar and the dedicated spiritual student. Her information is presented in an engaging style for easy reading, and yet contains well-researched, intriguing details. I highly recommend her books, and this book in particular, for those interested in learning more about Celtic spirituality and history.

Christy Nicholas, author of *The Druid's Brooch Series*

If I was a complete beginner at working with the Fairies, and I discovered this book on the Fairy Queens: It is an absolutely wonderful place to start. Don't be fooled, however, by the short-and-sweet length of this book, Morgan has packed every micro-inch with seemingly unending depth! And yet, here I was, reading along, easily accessing the material; able to immediately apply the lore-sourced recommended approach, demeanor, and excellent meditations. I regard Morgan, not lightly, as THE fairy expert of choice for the 21st century, and because of that, this book is quite fitting for even those advanced in this work. Well-done Morgan!

Lisa Allen (Calantirniel), Co-Founder of ElvenSpirituality.com, derived from the viewpoint of the elves in JRR Tolkien's *Middle-Earth* stories, author of over two dozen articles for the Llewellyn Worldwide, contributing writer for Moon Books anthologies *Paganism 101, Pagan Planet* and *Every Day Magic, a Pagan Book of Days*

Pagan Portals - Fairy Queens is more than the title might indicate. It is not only a look at the better known Fairy Queens, but also a practical system for maintaining fairy contacts, as well as concise, practical information on Fairy society, mores, and how best to work with this powerful, mercurial race. Readers can be sure, when they work with this book, that they are getting the best information available, that it will be clear, well-organized, easy to understand, and doable by the

average person. In short, I recommend this book very highly. Those seeking after the Fairy path need this book, and will gain much from it.
Segomâros Widugeni, author of *Ancient Fire an Introduction to Gaulish Polytheism*

Morgan Daimler's *Fairy Queens* is succinct introduction to these fairy monarchs. Packed with historical evidence and personal experiences, this book is the perfect stepping stone for anyone seeking to forge a deeper relationship with these enigmatic figures.
Nicholas Pearson, author of *Stones of the Goddess* and *The Seven Archetypal Stones*

"Daimler has taken some of the most interesting figures throughout fairy-lore and given them front and center space in the pagan community. This book gives a concise introduction to some of the most fierce members of the Fair Folk and gives the reader not only historical but also practical magical knowledge on each of these Queens. Daimler has a way with combing academia with modern spiritual experiences in a way that allows the reader to form their own well-rounded experience of these figures. This book is informative, practical, and a fantastic glimpse into the upper echelon of the Good Neighbors.
Aaron Oberon, author of *Southern Cunning: Folkloric Witchcraft in the American South*

If you are interested in connecting with the Queens of Faerie, this book is for you! Morgan gives thoughtful, hands-on techniques on working with The Good Folk, in an easy-to-read, conversational style. An absolute MUST HAVE for all those interested in learning about Faerie and connecting, on a deeper level, with the Faerie Queens! I love this book!
Michelle Skye, high priestess of the craft, women's empowerment facilitator, author of *Goddess Alive!*, *Goddess Afoot!*, and *Goddess Aloud!*

Pagan Portals
Fairy
Queens

Meeting the Queens of the Otherworld

Pagan Portals
Fairy
Queens

Meeting the Queens of the Otherworld

Morgan Daimler

Winchester, UK
Washington, USA

JOHN HUNT PUBLISHING

First published by Moon Books, 2019
Moon Books is an imprint of John Hunt Publishing Ltd., No. 3 East Street, Alresford
Hampshire SO24 9EE, UK
office@jhpbooks.com
www.johnhuntpublishing.com
www.moon-books.net

For distributor details and how to order please visit the 'Ordering' section on our website.

Text copyright: Morgan Daimler 2018

ISBN: 978 1 78535 833 3
978 1 78535 842 5 (ebook)
Library of Congress Control Number: 2018957880

All rights reserved. Except for brief quotations in critical articles or reviews, no part of this
book may be reproduced in any manner without prior written permission from the publishers.

The rights of Morgan Daimler as author have been asserted in accordance with the Copyright,
Designs and Patents Act 1988.

A CIP catalogue record for this book is available from the British Library.

Design: Stuart Davies

UK: Printed and bound by CPI Group (UK) Ltd, Croydon, CR0 4YY
US: Printed and bound by Thomson-Shore, 7300 West Joy Road, Dexter, MI 48130

We operate a distinctive and ethical publishing philosophy in
all areas of our business, from our global network of authors to
production and worldwide distribution.

Contents

This book is dedicated to all my friends who walk this path with me or who inspire me as I walk it. Especially to Mel, Vyviane, Lora, Angela, and Izzy.

My own journey in Fairy was not something I ever expected to intersect with a Fairy Queen, and yet it did. My own spirituality was not something I ever thought would one day focus on a Fairy Queen, and yet it does. I hope that this book may help someone else in finding their way.

Ar Aoibheall; fognam beus mu rígain. Atú i bith inso ocus i bith eile do echlach.

Introduction

The Fairy Queens are alluring and mysterious, sometimes easy to find yet often difficult to understand. Some were clearly Goddesses once, and are understood in folklore to be Queens of the Otherworld now, yet others have more mysterious origins and we know them only as Fairy Queens, or even euhemerized into mortals. Some appear to us only as literary characters, while others have sprung newly realized from modern folklore and pop culture. Some have names, others only titles. All have power.

Over the course of this book we will be exploring the history and stories of many of the Fairy Queens, particularly the Irish and Scottish ones, getting to know them through their folklore and traditions. We will also be reaching out to them in more practical ways through guided journeys, sacred space, and offerings. Those who are only interested in learning from the more objective perspective can of course skip those portions while those who would like a more subjective, personal experience are invited to reach out and connect directly to the Queens themselves. Each Fairy Queen is her own unique person and each one will respond differently – some perhaps not at all – to each seeker. Some will be more welcoming and others may be difficult or even hostile to deal with. It is best to go into each experience with no expectations for what response you may get but simply to let the experience be whatever it is.

Before we get into meeting the Fairy Queens themselves, one at a time and in a few groupings, its best to begin with some basics about Fairy and how to interact with the beings who exist there and who come to our world from there. It can be tempting to think of fairies, and the Fairy Queens, as much like humans or even as humans who simply live in a different world than ours but I would advise against this mindset. When we look at the folklore and the views held within cultures that still have a

1

deep respect for these beings – the places where they originate and where they are still remembered – we find that they are viewed with caution as beings who have a very different way of understanding things and reacting to things. While some of them may have origins in our world in many ways they are very foreign to us and part of why some people seek to nurture connections with them is because they can and will bless our lives with health and luck; conversely if offended they can cause great misery.

There are some basic and very important rules a person should be aware of when dealing with the Good People, and I advise anyone interested in pursuing such a path to do some research into traditional approaches to it. That said the Fairy Queens are not only members of Fairy to whom all the usual rules of Fairy interactions apply but because of their high placement in the hierarchy of their world they also come with their own set of rules. And because nothing in Fairy is ever going to be easy or straightforward some of the rules for the Queens contradict the usual rules that would hold true for dealing with fairies in general.

Basic Guide to Dealing with a Fairy Queen

1. *Manners* – manners with all fairies are essential but I can't emphasize enough how vital they are with the Fairy Queens. Sometimes people have a tendency to take an approach when dealing with the Fair Folk, be it in dreams, journeys, or when visiting their places in our world, that is best described as casual. I'm not sure that's a good idea even if we are talking about a lower level being but it is most certainly a very, very bad idea when dealing with any of the Queens. All I can do here is remind everyone that this isn't like a weekly visit to your family even if you feel like the Fey folk are family to you; the Queens are royalty and they are used to being treated like it. So, treat them with the maximum respect you can muster.

2. *Bowing* – I know some people get very odd about the idea of bowing to anyone or anything but trust me when it comes to the royalty of Fairy you bow. Or kneel. There are references from trial records of Scottish witches who said they dealt with the Queen of Elfame who mention, explicitly, being told to kneel when they were brought to the Queen's court. This isn't a point you argue, you just do it. File it under showing proper respect to the ruler of a group of people you really don't want angry with you.

3. *Accepting Food and Gifts* – one basic rule of fairy etiquette that I often emphasize is not to eat or drink anything given to you by a fairy and to be cautious about gifts which are often not what they seem. Certainly the caution is always a good idea, but in the case of the Queens if you are offered food or drink by them you take it and you eat it. They do not have the same reputation for tricking people with these things that other fairies do and being offered and accepting such hospitality may be a sign to others that you have some degree of royal favor (if you will) or are otherwise under that monarch's protection in some way. Which is a good thing. There will likely be some sort of repayment expected but as a general rule the monarchs of Fairy are more straightforward about this and upfront in their dealings. They make offers and explain what they want, and then give a person a chance to accept or decline.

4. *No is an Option* – you can always say no to anything that is offered or asked of you but be careful in how you say it. A polite no will be accepted much better than an angry refusal or rudeness. It's important though never to feel compelled or forced into anything. Because the Fairy Queens can be rather overwhelming to deal with its best to always go to their courts with a Guide, who can help you if you need it and advise you if you need suggestions on how to act or what to do.

Journeying to the Otherworld

One of the main ways that I recommend for connecting to the various Fairy Queens is by using guided mediations and journeywork. The two techniques are very similar but for my purposes here I tend to define a guided meditation as something that happens primarily within a person and is narrated by someone else; for example when someone reads you the script of a journey and you go into a meditative state and follow along to what they are saying. Generally speaking a meditation occurs within the mind and so you have total control over it. You can change things within it as you go by focusing on them, which is one quick way to tell if you are having a meditative experience. In contrast a journey is when you send a part of yourself outwards and into contact with other places and things. You don't have the same control over what happens in a journey because you are interacting with external beings that have their own personality and agency. Some people find they prefer either meditation or journeying and that's fine; both provide insight in different ways.

For our purposes here I'm offering a rough outline that could be used for either a guided meditation or for journeywork. In the case of journeywork the beginning will help get you where you need to go but don't be surprised if things go differently from there. Each subsequent chapter will end with a similar guided meditation/journey which will differ only in the details of the being you will encounter during the body of the journey. This repetition is useful to build the practice of journeying or meditation and to become more comfortable with the work being done and also, in my experience, is the best way to begin doing such work with Fairy beings.

It is best when doing regular meditations or journeys to keep a journal of your experiences. This can be an invaluable tool to check your progress and is also a great way to keep track of any messages or interactions you have with beings along the way.

I'm sure different people have their own approaches to this

4

and if you already have methods you use that work well for you, of course stick with those. For those who don't however, or who want to try some new things, I am going to offer a simple outline that can be used as either a guided meditation or journey. A couple quick tips for those less experienced with these methods: always have a mental out you can use if you need to get out of a situation quickly – this can include imagining a trap door for example – and never forget that you control when you go and when you leave; keep in mind that what happens in these experiences is as real as the waking world, from a spiritual perspective, so take it seriously and don't do or say anything you don't want to be held to; always go with a Guide.

Your Guide can help you in many ways as you travel in Fairy especially as you are first starting out. Your Guide will help you learn to discern those who may be helpful from those beings who could be dangerous to you. They will also help you be certain when you are going to meet the different Queens that the beings you encounter are the ones you are seeking. Fairy is full of tricksters after all.

Your first journey will be to meet someone who is willing to act as our Guide whenever you are traveling on these journeys. I highly recommend when you meet your Guide offering to give them something regularly as a token of thanks for their help. This could be pouring out milk or cream for them once a month before you journey, making a food offering on holidays, or paying them in silver coins before each journey. Whatever it is, be sure it's something you are willing to commit to doing.

Guided Meditation to Meet Your Fairy Guide

(It is best before doing this meditation to be certain you are comfortable with proper manners and etiquette when dealing with the Good Neighbors)

"Relax and breathe deeply...in and out...in...and out...

Feel the solid earth beneath you. Let your spirit move down, out, into the earth. Fill yourself with the energy that rests deep in the soil...When you feel empowered by this energy pull your spirit back up, out of the earth.

You find yourself sitting on the ground at twilight. Next to you is a staff of Rowan carved with symbols. The ground is warm beneath you, but the air is starting to chill as darkness falls. There is a light wind and you can smell the scent of a fire somewhere in the distance and of fallen leaves close by. You hear the sounds of birds calling to each other as they settle in to roost for the night and the murmuring of water over rocks. Although it is deep twilight and the world around you is dark you can see clearly. You are sitting in a field between an old forest and a river. At the other end of the field the shape of a hill rises up, a gentle curve in the earth.

As you look at the hill something catches your eye, flickering like firelight. You stand up, pick up the staff, and move towards the light...as you walk across the field towards the hill the light grows. As you get closer you can see that the light is coming from a door that opens up into the hill midway up the incline. Using the staff to help, you climb up the hill to the door.

At the doorway you are greeted by someone. A figure steps out of the doorway, a person who has clearly been waiting for you. This person will be your Guide in the Otherworld; take a moment to study them as they approach. What do they look like? What is distinctive about them?

Your Guide greets you warmly, "Hello! Welcome to the realm between. Where you are now is neither in your world nor in Fairy but in space between the two."

Your Guide steps back and gestures for you to enter. You carefully place the Rowan staff in the doorway to hold it open, and then enter the great room. Your Guide gestures for you to sit at a nearby table in a room full of firelight and people eating and drinking. They present you with a token, an item to wear or carry while you are there so that everyone will know you are a guest. This item is something that you may keep and wear every time you travel with this guide. Make sure to take some time to get to know your Guide; you may ask for their name but it is unlikely they will give anything but a pseudonym. You may want to ask if they are willing to go forward with you on your journey to meet the different Fairy Queens, and offer something you are willing to give them in exchange for their help.

(Allow time for whatever experiences you need to have)

When you have done what you need to do your Guide gently tells you it is time to leave. At the entrance you put your token somewhere safe and say farewell to your Guide before stepping out the door. You pick the staff back up and as you do the door closes and the doorway vanishes into the hill. You are standing alone on the fairy hill in the dark night. Carefully climb down the hill and walk back across the field. The night is silent now, and dark, and the wind is cold. Put down the staff and sit down, resting on the earth.

Feel the solid earth beneath you. Let your spirit move down, out, into the earth. Fill yourself with the energy that rests deep in the soil…When you feel empowered by this energy pull your spirit back up, out of the earth.

Return to your body; feel yourself solidly back in mortal earth.

Relax and breathe deeply…in…and out…in and out…

Move slowly, reconnecting to your body, until you are ready to open your eyes.

Write down everything you saw or experienced in your journal.

This has been your first introduction to the world of the Fairy Queens, both theoretically and through a guided meditation or journey. The Guide you met on this journey will accompany you on any future journeys.

Chapter 1

Navigating Elfland: Hierarchy among the Good People

In the Introduction we looked at some basic tips for approaching and dealing with fairies, which is an essential starting point. The next step, before we get into actually learning about and meeting each Queen, is to get an idea of Fairy itself and how things generally are among the Good People. While the etiquette from the last section was important because you need to understand how you, as a human, should approach the Queens, it's also important to realize that the Fey folk have their own hierarchy and rules among themselves which are different than those in play for humans.

Fairy is a world unto itself, or more truly several worlds, and as you journey into it to meet the Queens you need to keep a few things in mind. Firstly, time moves differently in Fairy so it's not uncommon to undertake a meditation or journey in which you feel like a short amount of time has passed only to find that when you return to the waking world it has been much longer than you expected, or inversely that it seems like a long time has passed for you but when you return it has been only a very short amount of time here. Secondly, as I mentioned in the Introduction, things that happen in Fairy in a meditation or journey are just as real as things that happen to us here and that means they have consequences. Not only do we need to treat the experiences as real and be careful of what we say and do, but you should be aware that it is possible to get hurt. Thirdly much like in our own world things can and do change while we are away. Even if you are going to the same places each time you visit don't be surprised if the place itself changes or the beings you encounter are different between visits. These shouldn't be massive shifts, hopefully, but some change is to be expected and is normal. The beings you encounter are real and exist whether you are around to interact with them or not.

Which leads us to the next point, and the title of this section, hierarchy among the Good People. Obviously we have already covered the idea that there is a monarchy and that those who occupy that upper echelon require the same respect that would be given to the most high powered of humans – if not more. However they represent the highest level of Fairy's inhabitants not the sum total of who can be found there. Fairy contains a diversity of beings that include a range from Kings and Queens to the most humble of beings, and everything in between. Humans tend to fall somewhere towards the lower end of that scale, particularly when we are in their territory. Never forget your place in that range and that the beings you encounter do not and will not all relate to you the same way.

When we are going there we will inevitably encounter these beings, across that whole range, and we need to keep in mind that respect is important and that we are not the rulers of this realm nor the most powerful things kicking around. Good manners, common courtesy, and humility are valuable here and I suggest approaching these experiences and the beings you will meet as you would if you were travelling in a foreign country here on earth, where the consequences of offending someone or breaking a law are severe and cannot be appealed. You generally want to stay on good terms with the beings around you, don't pick fights unless you have to, have a good idea of when you are most likely to be in danger (and how to handle it) as well as who is most likely to help you.

This is why I suggest getting a good feel for folklore before taking the step of starting to travel in Fairy. There are several decent books on the market that look at the different types of beings from a more Celtic perspective. The two main ones I might recommend starting with are Brian Froud and Alan Lee's 'Faeries' and Katherine Briggs' 'A Dictionary of Fairies'. Froud and Lee's book is more fluid in its approach but is invaluable for its illustrations which will help you get ready for some of the different things you may see. Brigg's book in contrast is better for getting one acquainted with the various beings in a more orderly fashion and with snippets of important folklore attached.

A Note on Fairy Courts

Throughout this book you will see the term fairy court used so its important to understand the different contexts and meanings that this term can have. In one sense it can be a very general term, drawing from the Scots word court meaning a group or assembly and simply implying a group of fairies, usually of a specific affiliation. In another sense however, and the meaning that we will use more often here, a court is the group of people who are in service to and living in a royal household.

When we talk about the Two Courts or about the Seelie and Unseelie Courts we are using the term in the general sense of a group. The Seelie Court may be understood as the grouping of fairies which are more generally benevolent towards humans and slower to anger. The Unseelie are those more malicious towards humans and more inclined to cause harm without provocation. Additionally the term Seelie Court or Seelie fairy is used sometimes as a euphemism like Good People or Fair Folk would be. However it's important to understand that while these terms are useful for understanding fairies they are not always literally applicable to all of them and there is no wide spread loyalty to one or the other among the fey folk. The terms originated in the Lowlands of Scotland and that is where they have the most functional use; outside of that we are mostly using them figuratively. The Irish Fairy Queens, for example, would not belong to either of these Courts.

A fairy court as we mean it when applied to individual Fairy Queens is the specific group of beings who would attend or serve a Fairy Queen or King; we see this use in ballad material and in some anecdotes. This may raise the question with some people of what exactly a royal court would be and how it would function and since people who decide to use the guided meditations or journeys may find themselves encountering the courts of different Queens this is important information. Here we will briefly discuss what exactly a fairy court would be and who would be included in it.

A fairy royal court, like a mortal one, represents - effectively - the royal household which includes a range of beings from family of the monarch to counselors, servants, courtiers[1], court officials, entertainers, ladies-in-waiting, courtesans, knights, heralds, doorkeepers, cupbearers, stable hands, and huntsmen (Pattie, 2011; C& MH, 2014). Ladies-in-waiting are often the wives of nobles attending court or sometimes widows of such nobles tasked with keeping the Queen company, entertaining her, and sharing court gossip with the Queen. The Queen would also have maidservants or handmaidens who were not nobility and were servants in truth that would handle her personal needs. Who was a part of the court and who wasn't could be a fluid concept but generally a person who was in regular - usually daily or nearly daily - contact with the royal family and made their home at the royal court may be considered a member of the court. The size of any court was dependent on the size of the kingdom and its power and influence.

Keep in mind that just being a member of the court did not mean having rank in it. Having rank within a court meant having a specific title and duty within that court relating to serving the monarch, and the system of rank as one may assume was hierarchical. Certain titles implied a great deal more power and influence than others, and some positions, like master huntsman or master falconer, where usually held by members of the nobility (C & MH, 2014). To quote the article *'Officers and Servants in a Medieval Castle'*: "*The presence of servants of noble birth imposed a social hierarchy on the household that went parallel to the hierarchy dictated by function."* (C & MH, 2014). This is referencing human royal courts however it applies equally to courts in Fairy; rank in a court is a matter equally of birth and function within the court itself, and everything is a matter of rank.

If this sounds complicated that's because it is, and no less so for Fairy courts than for human ones.

The ruling monarch has a court; the members of their court do not have their own courts because only the ruling monarch has the authority to make governmental decisions, military decisions, and judgements of law. So a Fairy Queen would have her court but her children and other close relatives would not have their own courts unless they are ruling monarchs in their own right of their own territory or have been given specific authority to rule as a representative of the Queen in a different location. In the same way, non-royal nobility do not generally have courts although in some rare cases they might depending on the degree of authority they have over their own territory.

One example of a Fairy court of the type we are discussing comes from the ballad of Tam Lin. When Tam Lin is talking to his lover Janet about how she can rescue him he tells her this:

Then the first company which comes to you
Is published king and queen;
Then next the second company that comes to you,
It is many maidens.
Then next the company that comes to you
Is footmen, grooms and squires;
Then next the company that comes to you
Is knights, and I'll be there.
- Tan Lin 39G (modern English)

What we are seeing described is the Fairy court riding out in procession in groups, with the royalty first, then the queen's ladies-in-waiting, then the more general retinue of servants, then the knights at the rear. This is fully in line with what we might expect of a royal court, although I would imagine other nobles riding along with the king and queen.

A fairy court, whether that of the Seelie or Unseelie Queen or any of the Irish Fairy monarchs, would be complex and include a variety of beings that were part of the ruler's household, from close family to servants who waited on the royal family, as well as the same range listed above from advisors to huntsmen. These are usually beings who would be in permanent or near permanent attendance on the royal family, with the exception of knights who may be sent out or assigned specific tasks that took them away from the court. We can look to Tam Lin as an example of this, as he was a knight within the Queen's court but had been given the task of guarding a specific well in the forest of Carterhaugh. Courtiers, especially nobles, may also spend part of their time away from court, but would generally be expected to spend most of their time attending to the Queen or King.

As you move forward into meeting the Fairy Queens and interacting with them you may also interact with their courts, either as they ride out or through visiting them directly. At the least understand that these courts would include the royal household as well as courtiers, and that rank within a court would be an intersecting matter of birth and function. Everyone in a court has a function which ultimately serves the monarch, and the court itself is both representative of the monarch's power and a tool to exercise that power. The Queen is not the only one that you have to be respectful towards, and as an outsider – even if you develop a strong relationship with one of the Queens – you should keep in mind the complicated situation represented by a court.

On Travelling in Fairy with a Disability
I want to start by saying, in case it's not obvious, that while some people find meditation or Journeying just isn't their thing (which

is fine) there isn't – as far as I'm aware – any physical disability that would stop a person from doing this. A person who is deaf is just as able to Journey as a person who hears; a person with limited mobility is just as able to meditate as a person who runs marathons. Sending our spirits out isn't based on physical ability, beyond the ability to focus and engage in the meditation or Journey itself.

Everyone who does meditative or Journeywork will have different understandings of it and perceptions of the experience. I can't make a definitive blanket statement about how this works for everyone under every circumstance, so ultimately I encourage people to experiment for themselves to get a feel for how you personally react to being in different worlds. I have found that there is no one-size-fits-all to this, and also that where you are going matters because different destinations have different rules. You may find that certain places feel more like this world and come with the same physical limitations, while others do not.

My own experience has been that physical limitations relating to mobility may or may not crossover during meditations/journeys. In some cases you may find that you can manifest whatever form or image of yourself you choose, even shapeshifting if you want to. However if you have mobility issues and they do show in the Otherworld then, as in the waking world, we just have do what we can; asking your Guide for whatever assistance or accommodations you may need is a good idea and part of what your Guide is there for. You can also create or visualize what you need for yourself to a degree, especially if it has a real-world counterpart. Objects, even created ones, often have spirits of their own particularly if they have had energy invested into them, even unintentionally through regular use. If you have something that helps with your mobility in the waking world, like a cane, walker, or wheelchair, you can bring that with you when you meditate or Journey if you need it. If you feel the object has a strong sense of spirit you might want to ask it if it's willing to help you in this way, and then it becomes a type of ally for you; I have done this with a walking stick I have. Just remember you will have to add the steps of bringing the item with you when start and taking it back out when you go. Another option would be asking for or creating a counterpart object in Fairy that would remain there until you need it.

When it comes to stamina or issues relating to how much of something you can physically handle doing, definitely pace yourself and don't push, as much as possible. That may take a little trial and error to figure out, which is why it's important to run through some of the basic meditation/Journeys in Fairy several times and take notes about how they go. When you talk with your Guide in the 'Getting to Know your Guide' meditation I would definitely be very clear about whatever might come up with this – part of the importance of having your Guide with you whenever you travel There is that they can help you in situations where you need it. So if you are mid-Journey and talking to someone likely to be offended easily and you have a human-moment where you get sick or physically can't do something they expect you to do your Guide should help explain the situation to the other being. This is a big part of why I emphasize building a good rapport with your Guide before we get into meeting the individual Queens. It's true that the Queens are not particularly gentle, some less than others, but they can appreciate genuine effort – just be sure to make that effort.

Don't make yourself sick trying to push too hard with these things. Fairy is timeless, and the sense of time there is fluid at best, so any sense of scheduling is usually more on our end than theirs. While we may feel a need to do things regularly and indeed it can be good for us to practice these skills consistently, unless we have an obligation to do something on a schedule it's alright to wait or push back a planned meditation or Journey if we aren't feeling up to it. Some people may find these Journeys invigorating or energizing, in which case I'd caution against the allure of wanting to do them too often; other people may find them draining in which case you need to be careful about spacing them out enough.

Everyone is unique in what they can and can't do and how much they can handle of this particular work. It can be really tempting to compare ourselves against the successes or failures of others, but that just isn't, or shouldn't be, how this works. Don't measure yourself against anyone else except yourself.

Getting to know Your Guide and Exploring Fairy

That all said, our ultimate point here is meeting each individual Fairy Queen, and before we do that it's a good idea to get to know your fairy Guide better and also to get a feel for travelling in Fairy. For people who are familiar with these things this may just be a refresher but for those who haven't done many guided meditations or journeys in Fairy it's good to get some practice in before trying to seek out the more powerful beings within it. I would suggest trying this meditation/journey a few times before moving forward to meet the first Queen in the next chapter.

You'll also notice as we go on that the formats used each time start and end the same way; this consistency is important. Especially for beginners this helps to train the mind and provide keys that aid in getting into and out of the proper places. I will always have you meet your Guide in the same place and enter Fairy in the same place, no matter where the meditation ultimately takes you. If you have more experience and find this is too limiting feel free to tailor the experience for yourself. The idea here isn't to view these meditations/journeys as written in stone but to use them as guidelines or jumping off points in your own practice.

First we will do a meditation to get to know your Guide better and then one will be offered for exploring Fairy. You can do both meditations as often as you would like, although I do suggest not pestering your Guide too much or too persistently; if you treat them as you would another human friend you will likely do well. Exploring Fairy however can be a limitless opportunity, just remember your etiquette and to treat the experiences as real.

Guided Meditation to Get To Know Your Fairy Guide

"Relax and breathe deeply...in and out...in...and out...

Feel the solid earth beneath you. Let your spirit move down, out, into the earth. Fill yourself with the energy that rests deep in the soil...When you feel empowered by this energy pull your spirit back up, out of the earth.

You find yourself sitting on the ground at twilight. Next to you is a staff of Rowan carved with symbols. The ground is warm beneath you, but the air is starting to chill as darkness falls. There is a light wind and you can smell the scent of a fire somewhere in the distance and of fallen leaves close by. You hear the sounds of birds calling to each other as they settle in to roost for the night and the murmuring of water over rocks. Although it is deep twilight and the world around you is dark you can see clearly. You are sitting in a field between an old forest and a river. At the other end of the field the shape of a hill rises up, a gentle curve in the earth.

As you look at the hill something catches your eye, flickering like firelight. You stand up, pick up the staff, and move towards the light...as you walk across the field towards the hill the light grows. As you get closer you can see that the light is coming from a door that opens up into the hill midway up the incline. Using the staff to help, you climb up the hill to the door.

At the entrance to the fairy hill you meet your Guide, the same one that you encountered in your last meditation. Your Guide greets you and welcomes you back into the hill again.

You enter and find yourself in a wide hall with a fireplace at one end, the fire burning low. There are several large tables in the room with low benches next to them but you and your Guide are the only people present. The room is quiet and peaceful, and your Guide gestures for you to sit at one of the tables.

Once seated you may ask your Guide any questions you have. ......(leave time here for discussion).....

When you have done what you need to do your Guide gently tells you it is time to leave. At the entrance you put your token somewhere safe and say farewell to your Guide before stepping out the door. You pick the staff back up and as you do the door closes and the doorway vanishes into the hill. You are standing alone on the fairy hill in the dark night. Carefully climb down the hill and walk back across the field. The night is silent now, and dark, and the wind is cold. Put down the staff and sit down, resting on the earth.

Feel the solid earth beneath you. Let your spirit move down, out, into the earth. Fill yourself with the energy that rests deep in the soil...When you feel empowered by this energy pull your spirit back up, out of the earth.

Return to your body; feel yourself solidly back in mortal earth.

Relax and breathe deeply...in...and out...in and out...

Move slowly, reconnecting to your body, until you are ready to open your eyes.

Write down everything you saw or experienced in your journal.

A Guided Meditation to Explore Fairy

"Relax and breathe deeply...in and out...in...and out...

Feel the solid earth beneath you. Let your spirit move down, out, into the earth. Fill yourself with the energy that rests deep in the soil...When you feel empowered by this energy pull your spirit back up, out of the earth.

You find yourself sitting on the ground at twilight. Next to you is a staff of Rowan carved with symbols. The ground is warm beneath you, but the air is starting to chill as darkness falls. There is a light wind and you can smell the scent of a fire somewhere in the distance and of fallen leaves close by. You hear the sounds of birds calling to each other as they settle in to roost for the night and the murmuring of water over rocks. Although it is deep twilight and the world around you is dark you can see clearly. You are sitting in a field between an old forest and a river. At the other end of the field the shape of a hill rises up, a gentle curve in the earth.

As you look at the hill something catches your eye, flickering like firelight. You stand up, pick up the staff, and move towards the light...as you walk across the field towards the hill the light grows. As you get closer you can see that the light is coming from a door that opens up into the hill midway up the incline. Using the staff to help, you climb up the hill to the door.

At the entrance to the fairy hill you meet your Guide, the same one that you encountered in your last meditation. Your Guide greets you and welcomes you back into the hill again.

You enter and find yourself in a wide hall with a fireplace at one end, the fire burning low. There are several large tables in the room with low benches next to them with a handful of people eating or talking quietly.

Your Guide leads in and through the hall towards another doorway, then stops and asks you if you would like to pass through the hill and into Fairy. It is up to you whether you feel ready to go further or would like to remain and talk with your Guide. If you choose to explore ask your Guide to go with you.

The two of you walk through the back doorway and down a long hallway. Many doors branch from the hall, but your Guide leads you past them until you reach the end of the hall and a larger door. Your Guide opens this door, and on the other side you see a wide expanse of land spreading out in front of you beneath a twilight sky. You step through the door and choose a direction to walk in, your Guide near your side.

......(leave time here for exploration).....

When you feel you are ready to leave tell your Guide and

they will help you find your way back. They take you back to the fairy hill where you entered and to the doorway. At the entrance you put your token somewhere safe and say farewell to your Guide before stepping out the door. You pick the staff back up and as you do the door closes and the doorway vanishes into the hill. You are standing alone on the fairy hill in the dark night. Carefully climb down the hill and walk back across the field. The night is silent now, and dark, and the wind is cold. Put down the staff and sit down, resting on the earth.

Feel the solid earth beneath you. Let your spirit move down, out, into the earth. Fill yourself with the energy that rests deep in the soil...When you feel empowered by this energy pull your spirit back up, out of the earth.

Return to your body; feel yourself solidly back in mortal earth.

Relax and breathe deeply...in...and out...in and out...

Move slowly, reconnecting to your body, until you are ready to open your eyes.

Write down everything you saw or experienced in your journal.

End Notes

1   Courtiers are almost a topic unto themselves to be honest. A courtier was a person who attended the ruler at court and could include members of the nobility, servants, secretaries, merchants, soldiers, clergy, friends of the ruler, lovers, and entertainers. They may or may not hold actual rank in the court depending on a variety of factors. What defined someone as a courtier was the amount of time they spent hanging around the royal court, whether or not they ever actually even interacted with the ruler.

Chapter 2

The Queen of Elfland

Now that we've gotten a basic idea of the etiquette and navigating Fairy, and have met and got to know our Guide, it's time to start looking at meeting the Queens themselves. We will take our time with this and from here on out each individual chapter will be a look at the mythology of a selection of the Fairy Queens, their preferences as far as I know them, and then a meditation to meet them. As we've already mentioned the meditation should be taken seriously and treated as if it is really happening.

To start we will meet the Queen of Elfland, a figure who appears in the folklore of Scotland from at least the 16th century. She is never given a name in the stories and ballads she appears in and can be an enigmatic figure but is nonetheless a powerful force and one with whom we can connect today. It is possible, as ubiquitous as this Queen is across folklore, that she is not a single being but a grouping of beings who all share a common title, however for our purposes here we will approach her as one personage.

In some of the references to her in Scotland she is called the Queen of the Seelie court specifically and so that is the approach I take to her. The seelie are the fairies who are most well-inclined towards humans and most likely to aid us (although they can still bring harm if angered) so this Queen is an especially good one to begin with. Whereas some of the other Queens are more easily offended or angered the Queen of Elfland is somewhat more lenient and less inclined to take offense if none is intended.

The Queen of Elfland in Folklore

This Queen in folklore is called the Queen of Fairy, Queen of Fairyland, Queen of Elfin, and Queen of Elfhame (under various spellings). In the stories and references we have of her she usually appears alone although sometimes she might have an unnamed king by her side, and she may appear in a procession of knights and courtiers, called a Fairy Rade. When riding she is often on a white horse, a sign of her rank, and descriptions of her say that she wears either green or white and always fine material. She is described as peerlessly beautiful, sometimes compared to the Christian Queen of Heaven, and her behavior may best be described as generally benevolent but unpredictable.

An enigmatic figure she traveled to the mortal world in some ballads and took young men who interested her, keeping them for a period of time, while in other stories she held court in Fairy itself. In the Ballad of Alison Gross she is out riding with the Seelie Court on Halloween when she finds a man who had been bespelled into the form of a worm; she takes pity on him and returns him to his former shape (Acland, 2001). In all cases she appeared to be a powerful and influential force.

The Queen of Elfland is known to have a keen interest in young human men, particularly although not exclusively musicians, and was known to actively take men into her service, often for seven years. In ballads the Queen of Elfland appears and either lures a young man into her service or offers him the chance to go with her for a period of time and paying him what she feels suits. Going with her is not always voluntary however and in the Ballad of Tam Lin, young Tam Lin tells his mortal lover when questioned that he had joined the ranks of Fairy after falling from his horse one day and being caught by the Queen of Fairies who took him *"in yon green hill to dwell"* (Acland, 1997). The mortal lover eventually wins Tam Lin away from the Fairy Queen after pulling him from his horse on Halloween and holding him through a series of transformations, earning the Queen's ire; the Fairy Queen claims that she loves Tam Lin, although it is unclear if she means this in the sense of a mother or sexually. In a similar ballad with a less successful end for the human protagonist, The Faerie Oak of Corriewater, the Queen of Fairies has taken a young man into her service as a cupbearer, paying him with a kiss; his sister tries and fails to rescue him. In the Ballad of Thomas the Rhymer, a man sees a beautiful woman riding on a horse and after calling her the Queen of Heaven she corrects him and say that she is in fact the Queen of Elfland (Acland, 1997). Thomas is asked to go with the Queen into Fairy and to serve her for seven years, which he does, and in return is paid with the gift – or curse – of prophesy and truth -speaking. In some versions of the story the Queen eventually came back for Thomas, sending white deer to lead him back to Fairy where he still remains. A Scottish witch, Andro Man, claimed to have had repeated sexual encounters with the Queen of Elfland, or as he called it 'Elphin' (Henderson & Cowan, 2007). This tie-in to sexuality is an interesting echo of what we see in the ballads where the Queen also uses sex and intimacy to bind men to her service.

It was not always young men who were taken however, and we also see the Queen interacting with other people for various reasons. In 'The Queen of Elfan's Nourice' a nursing mother is abducted and put into the Queen's service, with the promise that the woman will be freed if she nurses the Queen's child until the child reaches a certain age (Child, 1882). The Queen also appears in the Scottish witch trial documents, and several Scottish witches said they owed their allegiance not to the Christian Devil but to the Queen of Fairies. Isobel Gowdie, one of the most well-known Scottish witches, described the Queen of Fairy well dressed in white and claimed she had been taken into the fairy hill and given as much meat as she could eat (Henderson & Cowan, 2007). Meat was a luxury food and it may be that Isobel being fed as much of it as she could want was form of payment for her services. Accused witch Bessie Dunlop claimed that she encountered the Queen of Elfland when she [Bessie] was giving birth, and Alison Pearson was put on trial and accused, in part, for spending time with the *'Quene of Elfame'* (Henderson & Cowan, 2007). Many of these witches told in the trials of having been brought to Fairy to meet with the Queen or the Queen and King of Elfland and related things they had done or seen while there. These visits and the relationship with the Queen could involve being given knowledge of healing herbs and skills, and in some cases potentially of cursing and elfshot. Several of these witches said it was this Queen who directed them in their witchcraft and assigned them a fairy as a familiar spirit (Wilby, 2005).

Sex and sexuality play a role with this Queen: a kiss as either an element of binding or as payment features in both The Faerie Oak of Corriewater and Thomas the Rhymer, and the Scottish witch Andro Man mentioned sex featuring into his relationship with the Queen. We also see in the stories her ability to both bless and curse people, having the power to transform what she chooses. It is easy to get stuck on the more lurid aspects of this, however if give this deeper consideration we can perhaps understand the profound power that lies in sexuality and generative forces, which this Queen, Queen of the Seelie Court, uses so well and directs at her will to influence the physical world.

She often takes people, but usually with their consent and for a set amount of time which seems to have been agreed on beforehand. If she asks you if you want to go with her no is always an option. Those who are taken involuntarily can be won free with effort. She is a power that transcends humanity yet chooses to seek it out and interact with humans, for both good and ill.

Honoring the Queen of Elfland

One method I might suggest for connecting to the Queen of Elfland is to set up a wild altar, perhaps under a tree. For those who have no access to outdoor settings or can't for any reason do this an indoor or virtual altar is also acceptable; I'd suggest using the image of a tree at the back though. Creating an altar space in your mind does work if a physical altar is not a possibility at all, and I'd suggest visualizing it as often as possible.

On this space you can add anything you personally feel would be appropriate for this Queen. The only essentials are a tree, or tree image, and a place to leave offerings. Before you start the meditation I would suggest leaving an offering of either an apple, honey, or cream. The offering can be left outside with intention, or placed inside overnight then moved outside or poured out. The belief is that the substance or essence of the item is consumed and what remains is simply an empty container.

If physical offerings can't be made at all like this then I would at least try to pour out some clear water for her.

Journeying to the Queen of Elfland

Journeying to meet any of the Queens is an uncertain process. The script is written assuming they will appear – the truth is they may not and that's alright. If no one comes the first time try again on another day. If no one comes after several tries, maybe wait or accept that the particular Queen in question is choosing not to interact with you. If a Queen does appear she may not acknowledge you or speak to you, or she may have a great deal to say. There is no way to predict what will happen. Remember these are autonomous beings with agency and remember they do expect to be treated with respect.

It's also important to remember that not everything that presents itself as one thing may actually be that thing – appearances not only can be deceptive in Fairy they usually are. When you are seeking any specific being it's a good idea to go in with an idea of what measure you will use to be certain that what you find is what you are actually seeking. Of course you can always just ask directly if you can find a polite way to do so, as no fairy will lie verbally, but you want to walk a fine line there of not being rude. If you decide to ask a straightforward question then be very careful of the answer, you will almost never get a direct yes or no and you need to be sure that what you do get still works out to a yes. For example if you ask "Are you the Queen of Elfame?" a yes would be "I am the Queen True Thomas swore to and who Tam Lin once served" or "I am She who rules over the land between shadow and light" but a no would be "Some call me a Queen; my land is one that has no ruler nor rules". This does take some practice and experience but your Guide should help you here until you start to get a feel for it.

My advice before you begin this Journey is threefold: listen to whatever your Guide tells you; promise nothing and give nothing that you are not truly willing to lose; never forget for a moment who it is you are dealing with.

"Relax and breathe deeply…in and out…in…and out…

Feel the solid earth beneath you. Let your spirit move down, out, into the earth. Fill yourself with the energy that rests deep in the soil…When you feel empowered by this energy pull your spirit back up, out of the earth.

You find yourself sitting on the ground at twilight. Next to you is a staff of Rowan carved with symbols. The ground is warm beneath you, but the air is starting to chill as darkness falls. There is a light wind and you can smell the scent of a fire somewhere in the distance and of fallen leaves close by. You hear the sounds of birds calling to each other as they settle in to roost for the night and the murmuring of water over rocks. Although it is deep twilight and the world around you is dark you can see clearly. You are sitting in a field between an old forest and a river. At the other end of the field the shape of a hill rises up, a gentle curve in the earth.

As you look at the hill something catches your eye, flickering like firelight. You stand up, pick up the staff, and move towards the light…as you walk across the field towards the hill the light grows. As you get closer you can see that the light is coming from a door that opens up into the hill midway up the incline. Using the staff to help, you climb up the hill to the door.

At the entrance to the fairy hill you meet your Guide, the same one that you encountered in your last meditation. Your Guide greets you and welcomes you back into the hill again, leading you through the doorway and into the hill. You step through into the familiar hall you have visited before but this time your Guide leads you through and out into the wider world of Fairy.

You cross an open expanse of grass and enter into a greenwood following a wide path. Your Guide leads you on and on, until you reach a small clearing lined with trees. Your Guide gestures you forward and as you cross towards the trees a figure emerges from the far side. She is tall and regal, clad in green velvet with an attendant close by each hand holding the hem of her dress up so that it won't drag in the grass. Her grey eyes regard you coolly but without hostility.

(Take time here to experience whatever occurs and let the experience unfold organically)

When you have done what you need to do your Guide gently tells you it is time to leave. You politely say farewell and wait for the Queen to leave first. You are led back the way you came, all the way back down the path, through the trees, to the mound, and then through the mound. At the entrance you put your token somewhere safe and say farewell to your Guide before stepping out the door. You pick the staff back up and as you do the door closes and the doorway vanishes into the hill. You are standing alone on the fairy hill in the dark night. Carefully climb down the hill and walk back across the field. The night is silent now, and dark, and the wind is cold. Put down the staff and sit down, resting on the earth.

Feel the solid earth beneath you. Let your spirit move down, out, into the earth. Fill yourself with the energy that rests deep in the soil...When you feel empowered by this energy pull your spirit back up, out of the earth.

Return to your body; feel yourself solidly back in mortal earth.

Relax and breathe deeply... in...and out...in and out...

Move slowly, reconnecting to your body, until you are ready to open your eyes.

Write down everything you saw or experienced in your journal.

Chapter 3

Nicnevin, Queen of Fairies, Queen of Witches

Having met the Queen of Elfland in the previous chapter, now let's take a look at Nicnevin who some say is the Queen of the Unseelie Court. The Unseelie are the less benevolent and more dangerous group of fairies, but Nicnevin is also strongly associated with witches and besides her title of Queen of the Unseelie she was also called Queen of witches, meaning that she tends to have a fondness for witches who seek to engage with her. Seeking her out next will also provide a balanced understanding between the two Scottish Courts, and wrap up our study of the Scottish queens before we move on to the Irish ones.

Nicnevin In Folklore

One of the most interesting and obscure figures in fairylore is Nicnevin. She appears in folklore from the 16th century onwards as a frightening figure that was used by mother's to ensure children's good behavior, a witch and queen of witches, and a Fairy Queen. In modern understanding she is often depicted as a queen of the Unseelie Court of Scotland. The truth of her nature and associations is shrouded in mystery now and comes to us only in hints and obscure references.

The meaning of her name is unknown, although the official etymology says that it comes from Nic Naomhin the Gaidhlig for *"daughter of the little saint"*; a similar name NicClerith (daughter of the cleric) is given in the 17th century to someone said to be a close relative of Nicnevin (DSL, 2017). Other theories claim the name is NicNemhain, or daughter of Nemahin, connecting her to the Irish war goddess Nemhain. A commentator on Campbell also offers the alternate spelling of NicCreamhain, which he suggests comes from Craoibhean, 'little tree man', as the ultimate source for the name Nicnevin (Campbell, 1900). I personally favor the idea that it comes from Nic Cnàimhan, meaning daughter of the bones, but it's really all conjecture.

She first appears in writing in a 16th century poem by Alexander Montgomerie, where he describes her this way:

> *Then a ready company came, soon after close,*
> *Nicnevin with her nymphs, in number enough*
> *With charms from Caithness and the Canonry of Ross*
> *Whose knowledge consists in casting a ball of yarn...*
> *The King of Fairy, and his Court, with the Elf Queen,*
> *with many elvish Incubi was riding that night.*[1]
> (language modified to modern English from Scots)

This is interesting for several reasons. We are told that she appears with her nymphs - probably a general term for female fairies or maidens - in 'number enough', reinforcing a previous line that referred to her appearing with a "company". She has charms [read: spells] from Caithness and Ross, both counties in the extreme north of Scotland[2] giving us a geographic point for her. We are also told that her knowledge or skill consists in casting balls of yarn or thread, one might surmise possibly as a method of divination or enchantment. This is an interesting connection to the Gyre-carling, who was strongly connected to spinning, and who will be discussed in more depth later. The poem itself goes on to describe the Fairy Rade she is riding out with in dark terms mentioning that they are accompanied by many elvish Incubi which is a common gloss for dangerous fairies, and it says that she is riding with an unnamed Fairy King (Briggs, 1976). This connects her directly to the Good People and counts her among their number, as their Queen.

Sir Walter Scott describes her in more depth in this passage:

...a gigantic and malignant female...who rode on the storm and marshalled the rambling host of wanderers under her grim banner. This hag...was called Nicneven in that later system which blended the faith of the Celts and of the Goths on this subject. The great Scottish poet Dunbar has made a spirited description of this Hecate riding at the head of witches and good neighbours (fairies, namely), sorceresses and elves, indifferently, upon the ghostly eve of All-Hallow Mass. (Scott, 1831).

From this we see an association between Nicnevin and storms, and we see her compared to the Goddess Hecate, as well as called a witch and described as leading a troop of witches and fairies. In the 200-odd years between the two depictions her association with witches has gone from something perhaps hinted at with her skill at magic and charms to something blatant. In the same way the description of the host she rides with has intensified and become more obviously dangerous, with Scott describing them riding *'under her grim banner'*.

She is also associated in that quote with *'All-Hallow Mass'* [Halloween], however due to the calendar shift in 1752 which moved dates by 11 days when it went into effect she became strongly associated with November 11th, the old-style date of Halloween/Samhain. Because of this we see her being acknowledged on both the new and old dates of the holiday. I have seen people today calling November 11th 'Nicnevin's Night', and some people believe she rides out with her company between October 31st and November 11th[3].

Nicnevin is often identified as a witch, being called the "Grand Mother Witch"; her name was also used as a general name for powerful witches (Scott, 1820). In later witchcraft trials those accused were intentionally connected to the folkoric Nicnevin to solidify their guilt (Miller, 2004). There is evidence of at least three women in the witch trial records of Scotland with last names that were similar to Nicnevin who were accused and killed for practicing witchcraft. The connection of Nicnevin to witches is complex, with her being viewed as both a witch herself, and also the leader of all witches. By some accounts she was a human witch who was burned at the stake in 1569 northeast of Edinburgh, while others claim her as the Queen of witches (Miller, 2004). She is also explicitly called the Queen of Fairies by sir Walter Scott writing at the beginning of the 19th century and in Montgomerie's 16th century poem.

Nicnevin and the Gyre-Carlin are closely inter-related and possibly names for the same being. As sir Walter Scott says: *"The fairy queen is identified, in popular tradition, with the Gyre-Carline, or mother witch, of the Scottish peasantry. She is sometimes termed Nicneven."* (Scott, 1802). The connection to the Gyre-Carlin is a complicated one, because she may be a separate figure who also has overlapping witch/fairy connections or she may be Nicnevin by a different name; certainly the two have extremely similar characteristics and associations. The name Gyre-Carlin breaks down to gyre: 'hobgoblin, supernatural monster' and carlin: 'a witch, a crone'. The Gyre-Carlin herself - or perhaps themselves as they may be a category of being and an individual - is described as both a witch and a supernatural woman. She is most associated with the area around Fife, where it's said that housewives who don't finish their spinning before the end of the year will have their unspun flax taken by her (DSL, 2017). The Gyre-Carlin was not limited to this one location, however, with her lore found around Scotland and the Orkneys. She was connected to the fairies for both were known to steal or bewitch babies, and she was also thought in the Orkney Islands to live in the ancient neolithic mounds, as did the Fair Folk (Barry, 1867). The Gyre-Carlin was said to be especially active on Halloween [Samhain], New Years, and the time between Candlemas [Imbolc] and Fasteneen [Lent] (DSL, 2017).

Another description of Nicnevin, which directly conflates her with the Gyre-Carlin, comes to us from a 19th century source: "*... a celebrated personage who is called the GyreCarline, reckoned the mother of glamour, and near akin to Satan himself. She is believed to preside over the Hallowmass Rades and mothers frequently frighten their children by threatening to give them to McNeven, the Gyre Carline. She is described wearing a long grey mantle and carrying a wand, which...could convert water into rocks and sea into solid land.*" (Cromek, 1810).

Here we see Nicnevin - called McNeven - directly connected again to the Fairy Rades or specifically those processions riding out on Halloween/Samhain. We are also given a rare physical description of her wearing a *'long, grey mantle'* and are told she carries a powerful wand that can transmute earth to water and vice versa.

Nicnevin is a difficult figure to suss out. The meaning of her name is unknown and we see it in various forms thanks to the non-standard orthography of the day. Her true origins are lost to history, and she appears 400 years ago as a figure fully formed in folklore, described as leading witches and fairies through the darkness of Halloween night, her unnamed King at her side. She is repeatedly associated with witches, sometimes even said to have been a mortal witch herself, yet she is also clearly associated with the fairies and called their Queen. She rides out during liminal times of year and during storms, leading a cavalcade of *'sorceresses and elves'*, and she is described as *'malignant'* and powerful, explaining, perhaps, the modern description of her as Queen of the Unseelie Court. The references we do have to her imply that she held a significant position in folklore, yet we have no existing myths or stories featuring her. We are left instead only with hints and later writing that seems to assume she would be known and understood by the reader. A modern understanding then, must be built on what evidence we do have and on whatever else can be gleaned from local folklore as well as individual perceptions.

Honouring Nicnevin

A good way to begin honouring Nicnevin is to set up a small altar to her. In my own experience I have found that she has a more macabre aesthetic and I might choose to decorate an altar for her with a dark cloth, bones, and divination tools, as her name may be related to the word for bone and she has connections to divination. It would also be appropriate to use woven or knit items. As a queen of the Unseelie any artwork featuring those beings would be appropriate, and as a Queen of witches so would art or items connected to witchcraft.

For offerings to her I would suggest apples, baked goods, and milk. Halloween, Samhain, and the time between October 31st and November 11th may be especially good times to honour her.

Journeying to Meet Nicnevin

As we journey to meet Nicnevin, remember the advice you were given last time for meeting the Queen of Elfland and the other lessons you have learned so far. Nicnevin has a darker reputation and grimmer personality than the Seelie Queen and I would advise more caution with her, but if you stay with your Guide and follow their lead you should be alright. Remember not to make any promises nor commit to anything in these initial meetings.

"Relax and breathe deeply…in and out…in…and out…

Feel the solid earth beneath you. Let your spirit move down, out, into the earth. Fill yourself with the energy that rests deep in the soil…When you feel empowered by this energy pull your spirit back up, out of the earth.

You find yourself sitting on the ground at twilight. Next to you is a staff of Rowan carved with symbols. The ground is warm beneath you, but the air is starting to chill as darkness falls. There is a light wind and you can smell the scent of a fire somewhere in the distance and of fallen leaves close by. You hear the sounds of birds calling to each other as they settle in to roost for the night and the murmuring of water over rocks. Although it is deep twilight and the world around you is dark you can see clearly. You are sitting in a field between an old forest and a river. At the other end of the field the shape of a hill rises up, a gentle curve in the earth.

As you look at the hill something catches your eye, flickering like firelight. You stand up, pick up the staff, and move towards the light...as you walk across the field towards the hill the light grows. As you get closer you can see that the light is coming from a door that opens up into the hill midway up the incline. Using the staff to help, you climb up the hill to the door.

At the entrance to the fairy hill you meet your Guide. Your Guide greets you and welcomes you back into the hill again, leading you through the doorway and into the hill. You step through into the familiar hall you have visited before and your Guide leads you through and out into the wider world of Fairy.

You cross an open expanse of grass and enter into a dark autumn wood following a wide path. Your Guide leads you on and on, until you reach a small clearing lined with trees. The trees are in various stages of losing their leaves to autumn's changes, some are already bare and others are a riot of color. Your Guide gestures you forward and as you cross towards the open space a figure emerges from the far side. She is tall and regal, clad in a grey cloak and dress; around her you hear the rustling sound of many other beings although you cannot see then in the shadows. Her dark eyes regard you coolly but without overt hostility.

(Take time here to experience whatever occurs and let the experience unfold organically)

When you have done what you need to do your Guide gently tells you it is time to leave. You politely say farewell and wait for the Queen to leave first. You are led back the way you came, all the way back down the path, through the trees, to the mound, and then through the mound. At the entrance you put your token somewhere safe and say farewell to your Guide before stepping out the door. You pick the staff back up and as you do the door closes and the doorway vanishes into the hill. You are standing alone on the fairy hill in the dark night. Carefully climb down the hill and walk back across the field. The night is silent now, and dark, and the wind is cold. Put down the staff and sit down, resting on the earth.

Feel the solid earth beneath you. Let your spirit move down, out, into the earth. Fill yourself with the energy that rests deep in the soil...When you feel empowered by this energy pull your spirit back up, out of the earth.

Return to your body; feel yourself solidly back in mortal earth.

Relax and breathe deeply...in...and out...in and out...

Move slowly, reconnecting to your body, until you are ready to open your eyes.

Write down everything you saw or experienced in your journal.

End Notes

1   I've translated from the Scots for ease of reading here, the original is:
    "Then a clear Companie came soon after clos,
    Nicneuen with hir Nymphis, in nomber anew,
    With charmes from Caitness and Chanrie in Rosse,
    Quhais cunning consistis in casting a clew...
    The King of pharie, and his Court, with the elph queine,
    With mony elrich Incubus was rydand that nycht."

2   The two regions are separated by Sutherland, but otherwise represent the northernmost area of Scotland.

3   This is information I have gathered by talking to various people, and should be considered anecdotal or personal correspondence. I have found nothing in actual history or folklore to support this. That said I think there is a lot of

value in the modern practices that have sprung up around Nicnevin which is part of what spurred me to write about her.

Chapter 4

Áine, Fairy Queen of Munster

Now that we have looked at the Queens of the Seelie and Unseelie Courts let's turn our attention to the Fairy Queens elsewhere. While the model of the two courts can be very useful it is something we only see in Scotland[1]; when we look at the Queens in Ireland we find more subtlety and nuance and less clearly delineated benevolence and malevolence. And so rather than a general 'Blessed' and 'Unblessed' Court each ruled by a Queen and possibly her attendant king we find instead a variety of localized Queens who ruled over specific areas. One such Queen, and the one we shall be looking at now, is Áine of Munster.

Áine in Folklore and Mythology

Áine has a very complicated and even convoluted history in Ireland, appearing in many guises including a goddess, fairy Queen, and mortal woman taken into the sidhe. What remains consistent in all of her folklore is her association with the area around Cnoc Áine (anglicized to Knockainey) and Lough Gur. Cnoc Áine's full original name is Cnoc Áine Cliach, which O hOgain suggests is a reference to the area's older territorial name of Cliú, although I would point out that cliú is also a form of the word (clu) which means 'of good repute' possibly giving us another way to interpret the name.

Áine's name has a variety of meanings including brightness, splendor, radiance, fame, and swiftness, and she is often associated with the sun or fire. As a fairy Queen it was believed that she could bring blessing and prosperity to people, but her roots as a goddess also gave her sway over sovereignty and we see her both legitimizing kings and destroying kings in her stories. Different authors have suggested she may have connections to both the Morrigan and Anu, and MacKillop posits that she may be the origin of the English fairy known as 'Black Annis'. In folklore she was known take the role of a bean sidhe [anglicized banshee] for one of the human families associated with her, the O Corra, by appearing to keen when members of the family died (Smyth, 1988).

Áine's parentage is disputed and there is no clear answer to who her father in particular is. She is sometimes said to be the daughter of Manannán Mac Lir or else the daughter of Manannán's foster son Eogabail, a Druid of the Tuatha Dé Danann and fairy king (O hOgain, 2006; Ellis, 1987). Other sources say that her father is Fer Í [Yew Man] although he may have been her brother instead (MacKillop, 1998). No mother is listed for her; her sisters may be Finnen, whose name means 'white' and Grian, whose name means 'sun' (Monaghan, 2004; Ellis, 1987). Her husband may be Manannán or else a figure named Echdae (MacKillop, 1998; Smyth1988). Áine is also said to be the progenitor of several human families including the Eoganachta, Fitzgeralds, and Ó Corras.

Like many fairy Queens Áine is reputed to have love affairs with mortals as well as immortals. In one tale a warrior of the Tuatha Dé Danann named Ètar fell in love with her but died of a broken heart when she rejected him. The Eoganachta line was founded when Áine had a child by Ailill Olum, although stories differ as to how this child was conceived. The most common version has the king, Ailill, coming onto her hill on Samhain and when she and her father, Eoghabhal the king of that fairy hill, emerge Ailill and his poet killed the king and Ailill forced himself on Áine. In retaliation after being raped she bit off his ear, giving him his name of Olum [one ear] and swore to end his rule as king[2]. According to the story, the child of this union was Eogan whose line went on to claim rulership of the land through their descent from the Áine (Monaghan, 2004). Older versions, however, may have originally placed Ailill as Áine's consort in partnership and without any hostility found in the later versions (O hOgain, 2006).

The most well-known of Áine's human descendants is probably the third earl of Desmond, Gearoid Iarla [earl Gerald], who was her son by the first earl of Desmond. According to the story Maurice, first earl of Desmond, saw Áine bathing in Lough Gur one day and took her cloak which was draped nearby, thus gaining some power over her; the two lay together and Gearoidwas conceived (O hOgain, 2006). Interestingly in folklore Gearoid is said to have been taken eventually by his mother into the lake and MacKillop connects Gearoid to Welsh tales of the Gwragedd Annwn, or lake maidens. Some tales say that he lives still within the lake and can be seen riding beneath the water on a white fairy horse, or else appears every seven years to ride around the lake on a white horse, while still other stories claim that Áine turned him into a goose on the shore of the lake (MacKillop, 1998; Ellis, 1987).

Áine is said to take the form of a red mare, who sometimes travels around Lough Gur. She has also been known to appear to people on Cnoc Áine at midsummer in the form of a woman, once showing a group of girls a vision of the fairies gathered there to celebrate along with the humans who had come to the hill for the holiday. The hill of Cnoc Áine is one of the most well-known places associated with her, said to have been named after her during the settling of Ireland when she used magic to help her father win the area (O hOgain, 2006). It is still viewed by some people as her sidhe, or fairy hill, to this day. Additionally there is another hill called Cnoc Áine in county Derry, and a third in Donegal (O hOgain, 2006). In Ulster there is a well called Tobar Áine that bears her name.

Midsummer was her special holy day and up until the 19th century people continued to celebrate her on the eve of Midsummer with a procession around the hill, carrying torches of burning straw in honor of Áine na gClair, Áine of the Wisps

(Ellis, 1987). Áine is also sometimes called Áine Chlair, a word that may relate to wisps or may be an old name for the Kerry or Limerick area (Monaghan, 2004; O hOgain, 2006). On midsummer clumps of straw would be lit on her hill and then scattered through the cultivated fields and cows to propitiate Áine›s blessing (O hOgain, 2006). In county Louth there is a place called Dun Áine where people believe that the weekend after Lughnasa belongs to Áine, and in some folklore she is said to be the consort of Crom Cruach during the three days of Lughnasa (O hOgain, 2006; MacNeill, 1962).

Áine has been much loved, even up until fairly recently and there is a saying that she is *"the best hearted woman who ever lived"* (O hOgain, 2006). Her connections to both the Irish gods and fairylore are strong and inseverable from each other and it would be wise when approaching her to bear in mind both that Áine is extremely powerful and also that whether as a goddess, fairy, or local legend she has been – effectively – continuously acknowledged until the present day.

Honouring Áine

To connect to and honour Áine there are several things you can do. She is associated with both the hill of Cnoc Áine as well as Lough Gur; since many people won't be able to actually visit there you might set up a small altar featuring images of these places. You could also consider including earth, water, and fire on your altar to symbolize the different things that she is connected to. Midsummer is a particularly good time to reach out to Áine.

Personally I have had good luck offering cakes to her; milk and butter would be traditional more generally for offering to the Good People.

Journeying to Meet Áine

Áine has a somewhat more approachable and gentle demeanor than some of the other Queens and has been known over the years to engage with mortals, both as lovers and more casually. She is a good choice to reach out as you begin to get to know the named Queens, because of her personality, but never forget that she is both a goddess and fairy Queen and shouldn't be treated lightly, no matter how friendly she may appear.

As always my advice before you begin this Journey is threefold: listen to whatever your Guide tells you; promise nothing and give nothing that you are not truly willing to lose; never forget for a moment who it is you are dealing with.

"Relax and breathe deeply...in and out...in...and out...

Feel the solid earth beneath you. Let your spirit move down, out, into the earth. Fill yourself with the energy that rests deep in the soil...When you feel empowered by this energy pull your spirit back up, out of the earth.

You find yourself sitting on the ground at twilight. Next to you is a staff of Rowan carved with symbols. The ground is warm beneath you, but the air is starting to chill as darkness falls. There is a light wind and you can smell the scent of a fire somewhere in the distance and of fallen leaves close by. You hear the sounds of birds calling to each other as they settle in to roost for the night and the murmuring of water over rocks. Although it is deep twilight and the world around you is dark you can see clearly. You are sitting in a field between an old forest and a river. At the other end of the field the shape of a hill rises up, a gentle curve in the earth.

As you look at the hill something catches your eye, flickering like firelight. You stand up, pick up the staff, and move towards the light...as you walk across the field towards the hill the light grows. As you get closer you can see that the light is coming from a door that opens up into the hill midway up the incline. Using the staff to help, you climb up the hill to the door.

At the entrance to the fairy hill you meet your Guide. Your Guide greets you and welcomes you back into the hill again, leading you through the doorway and into the hill. You step through into the familiar hall you have visited before and your Guide leads you through and out into the wider world of Fairy.

You cross an open expanse of grass and enter into a greenwood following a wide path. Your Guide leads you on and on, until you pass out of the greenwood entirely and reach the shore of a wide lake. Your Guide gestures you forward and as you cross towards the shore a figure emerges from the trees near the edge of the water. She is tall and regal, wearing a green dress covered by a white cloak. Her eyes regard you thoughtfully as you approach and you can hear a goose calling in the distance.

(Take time here to experience whatever occurs and let the experience unfold organically)

When you have done what you need to do your Guide gently tells you it is time to leave. You politely say farewell and wait for the Queen to leave first. You are led back the way you came, all the way back down the path, through the trees, to the mound, and then through the mound. At the entrance you put your token somewhere safe and say farewell to your Guide before stepping out the door. You pick the staff back up and as you do the door closes and the doorway vanishes into the hill. You are standing alone on the fairy hill in the dark night. Carefully climb down the hill and walk back across the field. The night is silent now, and dark, and the wind is cold. Put down the staff and sit down, resting on the earth.

Feel the solid earth beneath you. Let your spirit move down, out, into the earth. Fill yourself with the energy that rests deep in the soil…When you feel empowered by this energy pull your spirit back up, out of the earth.

Return to your body; feel yourself solidly back in mortal earth.

Relax and breathe deeply…in…and out…in and out…

Move slowly, reconnecting to your body, until you are ready

to open your eyes.

Write down everything you saw or experienced in your journal.

End Notes

1 The two Courts specifically refers to the Seelie and Unseelie Courts of Scotland. Of course every Fairy Queen will have her own royal court that attends her, but the Scottish Courts are more properly understood as wider divisions of the fairies into the blessed [Seelie] and wicked [Unseelie] rather than royal courts specific to an individual Queen or Queens.

2 According to mythology she did successful cost Ailill his kingship eventually, fulfilling her promise to avenge herself against him.

Chapter 5

Aoibheall, Fairy Queen of Clare

The next named Fairy Queen we're going to look at is Aoibheall, who is also found in the southwest of Ireland like Áine. She is a more obscure Fairy Queen but her folklore goes back to at least the 11th century. She is found in Clare and some of the surrounding areas, and like so many other Fairy Queens in Ireland also has a reputation as a Bean Sidhe [banshee] and is known to interfere in human issues for both good and ill.

Her name is from the Old Irish word oibell for 'spark, flame, heat' and as an adjective means 'bright or merry'. There are many variants of the spelling of her name including Aoibhell, Aoibhil, Aíbell, Aebill, Eevell, and Ibhell; it is pronounced roughly 'EEval'. By some accounts her name was once Aoibheann [EEvan], which is said to mean beautiful or lovely, from the Old Irish oíbhan 'little beauty' (MacKillop, 1996). Understanding the meaning of her name gives us the first clue as to her nature and temperament.

Aoibheall in Folklore

She is not found named among the lists of the Tuatha Dé Danann, but we may perhaps see a connection there as by some accounts her sister is Clíodhna, and while folklore does not tell us about Aoibheall's parentage we do know that Clíodhna's father was Gabann, a druid of Manannán mac Lir. The two are also rivals, specifically over the affections of a man named Caomh; because of this rivalry at one point Clíodhna turned Aoibheall into a white cat.

In folklore Aoibheall is said to have control over the weather and she possesses a magical harp whose music kills those who hear it. Her harp may be why she is considered by some in more recent folklore to be an omen of death.

She was likely originally a territory and sovereignty goddess of Clare, associated with mortal kingship and succession, and is later known as a fairy queen and bean sidhe. Her sidhe, or fairy hill, is at Craig Liath [Craglea] which is also called Craig Aoibheall [Crageevel] (MacKillop, 1996). Nearby there is a well associated with her called Tobhar Aoibill. Her presence is connected to the area of Slieve Bearnagh and more generally around Killaloe. One later bit of folklore says that Aoibheall left the area after the wood around Craig Laith was cut down. She is often called the Fairy Queen of Tuamhain [Thomond] which was a historic territory of the Dál gCais that is now modern-day Clare, Limerick, and some of Tipperary.

She is known as the protector of the Dál gCais, and so the O'Briens, and she is called both their bean sidhe and the banfáidh ó mBriain [prophetess or seeress of the O'Brien's]. It is said that she appeared to Brian Boru in 1014 the night before the battle of Clontarf and predicted his death as well as who his successor would be; she was also said to be the lover of one of his sons Donnchadh although other accounts suggest her lover was Dubhlaing the attendant of his eldest son (O hOgain, 2006; MacKillop, 1996). According to folklore she tried to keep her lover, Donnchadh or Dubhlaing, from the battle by misleading him with a magical mist (Dinneen, 1900; O hOgain, 2006).

She appears as the judge in Merriman's 18th century poem An Cuirt an Mhéan Oíche, hearing the complaint of women, that men do them wrong in not marrying them and taking advantage of them. In that poem she is called "*the truthful*" and "*all-seeing*". She sides with the women, ruling that men must marry by 21 or are open to women's reprisals. In a poem by Aodhagháin Uí Rathaillle Aoibheall is one of three fairy women travelling among various sidhe who lit three candles on Cnoc Firinne to welcome a king (Dinneen, 1900). The poet describes her as hooded, truthful, and '*not dark of aspect*'; in another poem he calls her '*chalk-white*'

(Dinneen, 1900). She also appears in the folk song An Buachaill Caol Dubh where she asks the spirit of alcohol, personified as a *'dark, slim boy'*, to release a person under his sway.

Of all the Queens Aoibheall is the one I am personally the closest to. I find her to be as capricious and mercurial as any of the aos sidhe but also both more openly joyous and quick to anger than others I have encountered. I have seen her with both red and blond hair; folklore doesn't describe her hair colour, only that she is likely not dark haired and very pale. She has no known king in folklore, but we may perhaps assume a fondness for poets and musicians, although I have personally found her to be a bit hard towards men.

Aoibheall is a complex folkloric figure. Her actions in poem and song seem benevolent, yet in folklore she is associated with death, both through its prediction and causing it with her harp music. Like many Fairy Queens she takes human lovers, and we might associate her with cats, especially white ones, and with fire. Like the flame itself she is named beautiful, yet can be either terribly destructive or a great blessing. Ultimately she is as much mystery as certainty.

Honouring Aoibheall

A small altar or shrine can be set up for Aoibheall including both fire and water, perhaps in the form of a candle and small bowl of fresh water. A white cloth may be appropriate. You could also have a small plate to leave offerings; I recommend with this Queen especially to try to focus on the best quality you can manage.

I have found that it works well to use the cat as her symbol, and white or grey work well for her colours.

Offerings to her might include anything from the traditional cream, honey, or baked goods, to music or poetry. If being left outside I have found she prefers them left on rocks rather than near trees, but that may be different for different people.

Journeying to Meet Aoibheall

Aoibheall is the second named Queen and the fourth Queen you will be journeying to meet. I would offer this word of caution before you try this meditation: unlike the others, including Nicnevin, Aoibheall can be difficult to deal with and tends to be less welcoming to men. She is definitely a Queen you will need to be on your best behaviour with and I encourage you to keep in mind what you have learned in your previous experiences. More so than the others I really recommend making an effort to get to know her first with offerings and some quite meditation, to get a feel for who she is before you reach out to meet her 'in person' as it were.

As always: listen to whatever your Guide tells you; promise nothing and give nothing that you are not truly willing to lose; never forget for a moment who it is you are dealing with.

"Relax and breathe deeply…in and out…in…and out…

Feel the solid earth beneath you. Let your spirit move down, out, into the earth. Fill yourself with the energy that rests deep in the soil…When you feel empowered by this energy pull your spirit back up, out of the earth.

You find yourself sitting on the ground at twilight. Next to you is a staff of Rowan carved with symbols. The ground is warm beneath you, but the air is starting to chill as darkness falls. There is a light wind and you can smell the scent of a fire somewhere in the distance and of fallen leaves close by. You hear the sounds of birds calling to each other as they settle in to roost for the night and the murmuring of water over rocks. Although it is deep twilight and the world around you is dark you can see clearly. You are sitting in a field between an old forest and a river. At the other end of the field the shape of a hill rises up, a gentle curve in the earth.

As you look at the hill something catches your eye, flickering like firelight. You stand up, pick up the staff, and move towards the light...as you walk across the field towards the hill the light grows. As you get closer you can see that the light is coming from a door that opens up into the hill midway up the incline. Using the staff to help, you climb up the hill to the door.

At the entrance to the fairy hill you meet your Guide. Your Guide greets you and welcomes you back into the hill again, leading you through the doorway and into the hill. You step through into the familiar hall you have visited before and your Guide leads you through and out into the wider world of Fairy.

You cross an open expanse of grass and enter into a greenwood following a wide path. Your Guide leads you on and on, up a slight incline. You pass an old natural well, the water bubbling up surrounded by well-worn rocks. You continue as the incline gets steeper and the path winds up the hill. The trees around you sway slightly in a breeze. You reach the top of a hill, and the trees thin out into a small grove. Your Guide gestures you forward and as you cross towards the open space a figure emerges from the far side. She is well-formed and bold in her movements, clad in a white dress and accompanied by a small white cat. Her blond hair falls in waves to her waist and her green eyes give you a long measuring look.

(Take time here to experience whatever occurs and let the experience unfold organically)

When you have done what you need to do your Guide gently tells you it is time to leave. You bow to the Queen and slowly back out of the grove then retrace your steps down the hill. Your Guide leads you back through the woods, past the well, across the open grass and back into the hill you first entered. You pass back through the now familiar hill and to the same place you originally entered. At the entrance you put your token somewhere safe and say farewell to your Guide before stepping out the door. You pick the staff back up and as you do the door closes and the doorway vanishes into the hill. You are standing alone on the fairy hill in the dark night.

Carefully climb down the hill and walk back across the field. The night is silent now, and dark, and the wind is cold. Put down the staff and sit down, resting on the earth.

Feel the solid earth beneath you. Let your spirit move down, out, into the earth. Fill yourself with the energy that rests deep in the soil...When you feel empowered by this energy pull your spirit back up, out of the earth.

Return to your body; feel yourself solidly back in mortal earth.

Relax and breathe deeply...in...and out...in and out...

Move slowly, reconnecting to your body, until you are ready to open your eyes.

Write down everything you saw or experienced in your journal.

Chapter 6

Cliodhna Fairy Queen and Bean Sidhe

Clíodhna (old Irish Clíodna – pronounced KLEEuhn-uh) is a Fairy Queen and is also sometimes counted among the Tuatha Dé Danann of Ireland. The meaning of her name is uncertain but may be '*the territorial one*', likely reflecting her earlier role as a sovereignty Goddess associated with the province of Munster and especially with Cork (O hOgain, 2006). She formed a triad of such deities with Áine and Aoibheall who we have previously discussed and all three are now understood as Fairy Queens showing that while how people understand them may have changed, their importance remains. In modern folklore she is the Queen of the Munster fairies, and one poet in the mid-19th century refers to '*the troops of Clíodhna*' in a poem about fairies pursuing a human in revenge over a death (Carraig Cliona, 2018; O'Kearny, 1855).

Cliodhna in Folklore

Clíodhna's epithet is Ceannfhionn (fair headed or fair haired) and she is sometimes called '*the shapely one*' (O hOgain, 2006; MacKillop, 1998). In many stories she is described as exceptionally beautiful. She has a reputation in many stories for her passionate nature and love of poets in particular, and in later folklore, when she is considered a Fairy Queen, she is known to abduct handsome young poets or to appear and try to seduce them. In folklore she has a reputation for seducing and drowning young men (Smyth, 1988). Several mortal families trace their descent from her including the McCarthys and O'Keefes and she was well known for taking mortal lovers.

There are no references to who her mother might be or to her children among the Gods, but we know her sister is Aoibheall, and her father is said to be Gebann, the Druid of Manannán mac Lir (Smyth, 1988; MacKillop, 1998). In one story Clíodhna and Aoibheall were both in love with the same mortal man; he favoured Aoibheall so Clíodhna used magic to first sicken Aoibheall and then turn her into the form of a white cat so that the man would choose her instead, which he did (O hOgain, 2006).

She is often connected to the Otherworldly bean sidhe – anglicized as banshee - the fairy woman who is attached to certain families and who appears before a death in that family to cry and keen for the dying person. By some accounts she herself is considered to be such a spirit, as is her sister Aoibheall, and she is also known as the queen of all banshees. Banshee folklore is rich and unique, often misunderstood, and like Clíodhna herself the folklore of these spirits shows a likely shift from sovereignty goddesses protecting important families and mourning the deaths of leaders to Otherworldly figures who are omens of death (O hOgain, 2006).

She has three magical birds that eat Otherworldly apples and have the power to lull people to sleep by singing and then heal them (Smyth, 1988; MacKillop, 1998). In another story Cliodhna took the form of a wren, a bird that may be associated with her. The banshee is also associated with birds, at least in so far as she is said to take the form of a bird in some folklore, perhaps another layer of connection between Clíodhna and those Otherworldly spirits.

Clíodhna lives at Carraig Chlíona [Cliodhna's rock] in Cork as well as a wave at Glendore; both might be seen as entries to the Otherworld. Her stone in Cork is said to be so hard that even iron drills couldn't pierce it (Carraig Cliona, 2018). She is strongly associated with the shore and with waves, and the tide at Glandore in Cork was called Tonn Chliodna 'Wave of Cliodhna' (O hOgain, 2006). In several of her stories the wave was given its name because she is drowned at that location after leaving the Otherworld either to try to woo Aengus mac ind Óg or after running away with a warrior named Ciabhán.

Clíodhna is one of the more obscure deities among the Tuatha De Danann and modern pagans who choose to honour her may look to her as a sovereignty Goddess or as an ancestral deity related to specific families but it's important to understand her role as a Fairy Queen. Clíodhna's more recent folklore and her place as a Queen of the fairies of Munster is an important part of who she is, just as those seeking to connect to her as a Fairy Queen need to also understand her role as a Queen of the Banshees. Every layer of Clíodhna's history and each of her roles matters as we seek to understand who she was and is.

Honouring Cliodhna

An altar to Clíodhna could be decorated either with sea imagery or with things relating to the earth, like stones and wood. Because she is also known to take the form of a bird and to have birds around her you might want to use imagery related to that as well. For example if you were focusing on Cliodhna more as a Fairy Queen you might focus on her ocean aspects while if you wanted to connect to her healing qualities birds would be a better way to go, and as a bean sidhe you might choose a combination of birds and earth.

Offerings to her could include the traditional milk or bread. I have also had success offering her clear fresh water, whiskey, and treats like cakes and cookies. Whatever you offer should be given sincerely and with pure intentions.

Journeying to Meet Cliodhna

Remember that Cliodhna, like her sister Aoibheall, can be tempestuous and as unpredictable as the sea. As with several of the other Fairy Queens Clíodhna requires a bit of extra caution in dealing with, particularly if you are someone who falls into a demographic she is known to be prone to taking, including poets. Before you begin the journey, take a moment to settle yourself and focus on what you would like to gain in meeting this Queen.

"Relax and breathe deeply...in and out...in...and out...

Feel the solid earth beneath you. Let your spirit move down, out, into the earth. Fill yourself with the energy that rests deep in the soil...When you feel empowered by this energy pull your spirit back up, out of the earth.

You find yourself sitting on the ground at twilight. Next to you is a staff of Rowan carved with symbols. The ground is warm beneath you, but the air is starting to chill as darkness falls. There is a light wind and you can smell the scent of a fire somewhere in the distance and of fallen leaves close by. You hear the sounds of birds calling to each other as they settle in to roost for the night and the murmuring of water over rocks. Although it is deep twilight and the world around you is dark you can see clearly. You are sitting in a field between an old forest and a river. At the other end of the field the shape of a hill rises up, a gentle curve in the earth.

As you look at the hill something catches your eye, flickering like firelight. You stand up, pick up the staff, and move towards the light...as you walk across the field towards the hill the light grows. As you get closer you can see that the light is coming from a door that opens up into the hill midway up the incline. Using the staff to help, you climb up the hill to the door.

At the entrance to the fairy hill you meet your Guide. Your Guide greets you and welcomes you back into the hill again, leading you through the doorway and into the hill. You step through into the familiar hall you have visited before and this time your Guide leads you through and out into the wider world of Fairy.

You cross an open expanse of grass and enter into a greenwood following a wide path. Your Guide leads you on and on, through the forest as it grows thicker and then begins to thin. You keep moving forward, your Guide close by your side, as the trees slowly give way and finally open up to shoreline. To each side of you a beach spreads out, the sand meeting the tree line and stretching down to the waves.

Your Guide gestures you forward and as you cross towards the water there is a particularly large wave that sends white water crashing upwards towards you – instinctively you pause and throw your hands up to cover your face. When you look again there is a woman standing in front of you. She is tall and regal, clad in a dress that is all the shades of blue of the ocean. She tilts her head and looks at you thoughtfully, her eyes thoughtful.

(Take time here to experience whatever occurs and let the experience unfold organically)

When you have done what you need to do your Guide gently tells you it is time to leave. You politely tell Cliodhna that you appreciate the time she's taken to speak with you before backing up towards the trees. You don't turn your back until she has left first, then you return to the forest path and begin moving back towards the hill where you entered. The trees grow thicker around you as you walk, the shoreline falling behind you. Eventually you emerge and find yourself at the open field that will take you back to the hill. You cross the green grass and return to the familiar doorway. Your Guide leads you back through the hill, through the hall, and to the doorway where you first entered.

At the entrance you put your token somewhere safe and say farewell to your Guide before stepping out the door. You pick the staff back up and as you do the door closes and the doorway vanishes into the hill. You are standing alone on the fairy hill in the dark night. Carefully climb down the hill and walk back across the field. The night is silent now, and dark, and the wind is cold. Put down the staff and sit down, resting on the earth.

Feel the solid earth beneath you. Let your spirit move down, out, into the earth. Fill yourself with the energy that rests deep in the soil...When you feel empowered by this energy pull your spirit back up, out of the earth.

Return to your body; feel yourself solidly back in mortal earth.

Relax and breathe deeply...in...and out...in and out...

Move slowly, reconnecting to your body, until you are ready to open your eyes.

Write down everything you saw or experienced in your journal.

Chapter 7

Una, Fairy Queen of Tipperary

The last of the named Irish fairy Queens that we are going to look at in detail is Una, although there are of course more than the few I have presented here. I would encourage you to explore more of the folklore on your own if you feel like you still haven't found a particular Queen that really connects to you but you would like to. Of course it's also fine if you aren't looking for that and have just been curious about meeting them or learning more about them.

I am choosing to spell her name her as Una, but you will find variations in the spelling including Eabhna, Oona, and Oonagh. I am going with Una for two main reasons: it's one of the more common spellings you will find in the older material and the pronunciation is fairly obvious, I think. All of the various spellings are pronounced more or less the same way, roughly as EW-nuh

Una in folklore

Una is described as a peerless beauty, with shining golden hair that sweeps the ground and a silver dress that sparkles as if it were covered in crystal (Briggs, 1976). She is usually viewed as the wife of Fionnbheara, whose place is at Cnocmeadha, although she has her own abode elsewhere. She is said to have seventeen children, all sons (MacKillop, 1998). She is also known in stories to be a shape shifter and to appear in various forms including a black cat and a white cow.

The main site associated with her is in Tipperary and is called Knockshigowna today. 19th century sources suggest the name in Irish would be Cnoc-sidhe-una, or 'hill of the fairy mound of Una' (Joyce, 1869). However the name today is more commonly given as Cnocsíghabhna which may mean 'hill of the fairy cattle pen' or alternately as cnocsigamhna, 'hill of the fairy calf' (logainm. ie, 2018; Ryan, 2016). This confusion may be due in part to sighe being an older variant spelling of sidhe and Eabhna being one spelling of Una's name. This could give us, potentially, Cnoc sighe Eabhna which losing the doubled 'e' becomes Cnoc sigh abhna and then misunderstood as Cnoc si gabhna. What isn't disputed is that the word 'sí' [older spelling sidhe] or fairy hill is part of the name and that local folklore strongly associates it with Una.

Joyce describes Una's fairy hill as "*a noted haunt of fairies*" and says "*the whole neighbourhood teems with fairy names and fairy legends about Una*" (Joyce, 1869). There are a wide array of stories about the hill and the surrounding area, from the consequences to people who try to violate fairy privacy by spying on their revels to those who are punished for trying to cultivate lands claimed by fairies (Duchais.ie, 2018). These stories are in line with wider folklore about the Good People found throughout Ireland but do reinforce that Una's sidhe was known to be quite active even into the last hundred years. Despite the normal prohibitions against trespassing on the hill, especially after dark, there was a tradition of going there on Lughnasa to gather berries (McNeill, 1962).

Like some of the other Queens we've previously discussed Una was associated with specific mortal families, particularly the O'Carrolls (Joyce, 1869). She is sometimes considered a bean sidhe, in the traditional sense of a fairy woman who would appear and keen for members of the family she watched over. It is likely that she was an ancestor of the O'Carrolls and still feels connected to the descendants of that family line.

There's one particular story about Una that I heard a long time ago that I really enjoyed so I wanted to share it here. It can be found in various, slightly different versions, online and in books although I'm paraphrasing this version from Croker's 1834 work '*Fairy Legends and Traditions of the South of Ireland*'. I think it sums up her personality fairly well.

Once there was a farmer and he had a pasture near the top of Knockshigowna, where he would send his cows and a herdsman to watch them. But this place belonged to the Good People, and their Queen Una was angry that their dancing ground was trampled by hooves and full of the sad sound of cows lowing. So Una set about to drive the cows and herdsman away, and this was how she did it – she would appear at night to the herdsman, when they sky was full dark and he was relaxing back, and she would take on a series of hideous forms. She would seem to be a blend of different animals and like no animal on earth, and she would shriek and hiss and cry so that the cows ran about terrified and the herdsman prayed to the saints for help. But no help would come and the herdsman was held by her power so that he could neither flee nor hide. Because of this the cows were in a bad state, and often injured or killed besides, and the farmer could not keep a herdsman in his employ for they would all quit rather than go back to the pasture. The fairies rejoiced at this success and to have their pasture back but the farmer feared he'd lose everything if he couldn't pay his rent when it came due. He offered triple wages but still no one would take the work. Finally one day the farmer came across a piper who was renowned for his skill with music and his love of whiskey, and it was widely known that this piper when drinking would face the devil himself. The farmer shared his troubles and the piper bragged that even if there were as many fairies on the hill as there were flowers in a blooming field he would face them. The farmer promised a rich reward if the piper would watch the herd for a full week and a bargain was struck. The first night came and the piper set down and began playing, and he kept playing even as Una tried all of her terrifying shapes and noises on him. Finally, frustrated she changed into a beautiful white calf, thinking to trick him with a fair form. When she approached the piper quickly dropped his instrument and leaped on her back and she just as swiftly leaped in the air ten miles away to a different hill then kicked her heels up and threw him off. Landing on the ground the piper laughed and then turned to the Queen and said 'well done! That was quite a leap for a calf!' The Queen resumed her true shape and asked him if he would return as he'd arrived to which he replied yes, so she turned back into a calf and the two leaped back to Knockshigowna. When they arrived Una turned to herself again and she told the piper that for his great courage he would be rewarded, that he could keep cows in that field as long as he lived and none of Una's people would bother him. And so he did, piping and drinking at the farmer's expense and keeping an eye on the cows.

Honouring Una

An altar for Una could be decorated with a green cloth and with imagery from nature. I have found that she seems fond of beautiful things, particularly bright and shiny ones, but I'd caution against using imitation or plastic jewellery. As with all the Queens quality often comes into play and a single genuine item is better than a dozen low quality ones. That's not to say bankrupt yourself making an altar for her, just to consider what exactly you are putting on her space. I've found checking out antique stores and flea markets can work well on a budget. Also keep in mind less is often more in this cases.

Offerings to Una I would recommend milk or cream, fresh water, or small, sweet cakes. Feel free to experiment a bit here however as she does admire courage and as long as you don't try anything totally inappropriate I'm sure you'd get a sense of whether she approves or not.

Journeying to Meet Una

I organized the named Queens alphabetically simply for convenience, but I am glad that it works out so that you are Journeying to meet Una last. In my experience Una is one of the gentler Queens and has a good sense of humour, making her a fitting personage to round out our visits with. Although she can be fierce when she's annoyed she is also generous and willing to engage with humans in my experience.

"Relax and breathe deeply...in and out...in...and out...

Feel the solid earth beneath you. Let your spirit move down, out, into the earth. Fill yourself with the energy that rests deep in the soil...When you feel empowered by this energy pull your spirit back up, out of the earth.

You find yourself sitting on the ground at twilight. Next to you is a staff of Rowan carved with symbols. The ground is warm beneath you, but the air is starting to chill as darkness falls. There is a light wind and you can smell the scent of a fire somewhere in the distance and of fallen leaves close by. You hear the sounds of birds calling to each other as they settle in to roost for the night and the murmuring of water over rocks. Although it is deep twilight and the world around you is dark you can see clearly. You are sitting in a field between an old forest and a river. At the other end of the field the shape of a hill rises up, a gentle curve in the earth.

As you look at the hill something catches your eye, flickering like firelight. You stand up, pick up the staff, and move towards the light...as you walk across the field towards the hill the light grows. As you get closer you can see that the light is coming from a door that opens up into the hill midway up the incline. Using the staff to help, you climb up the hill to the door.

At the entrance to the fairy hill you meet your Guide. Your Guide greets you and welcomes you back into the hill again, leading you through the doorway and into the hill. You step through into the familiar hall you have visited before and your Guide leads you through and out into the wider world of Fairy.

You cross an open expanse of grass and enter into a greenwood following a wide path. Your Guide leads you on and on, the path wending upwards. You realize that you are walking up a hill. You continue through the trees, moving slowly upwards until you reach the crest of the hill and a small clearing.

Your Guide gestures you forward and as you cross into eth open space a figure emerges from the far side. She is beautiful, her blond hair falling like a curtain to the hem of her dress, which is a shimmering silver. She watches you with an amused expression to see what you will do next. Behind her you hear the sound of low voices talking in the trees, and know that she has come accompanied by her people.

(Take time here to experience whatever occurs and let the experience unfold organically)

When you have done what you need to do your Guide gently tells you it is time to leave. You bow to the Queen and then step back carefully into the trees, turning to make your way back down the hill. The path leads you down and down, the trees close on each side. Finally the greenwood path opens up into the wild field you first crossed and you cross it again to return back to the hill you started from. Your Guide leads you back through the hill and hall to the entrance you arrived at.

At the entrance you put your token somewhere safe and say farewell to your Guide before stepping out the door. You pick the staff back up and as you do the door closes and the doorway vanishes into the hill. You are standing alone on the fairy hill in the dark night. Carefully climb down the hill and walk back across the field. The night is silent now, and dark, and the wind is cold. Put down the staff and sit down, resting on the earth.

Feel the solid earth beneath you. Let your spirit move down, out, into the earth. Fill yourself with the energy that rests deep in the soil...When you feel empowered by this energy pull your spirit back up, out of the earth.

Return to your body; feel yourself solidly back in mortal earth.

Relax and breathe deeply...in...and out...in and out...

Move slowly, reconnecting to your body, until you are ready to open your eyes.

Write down everything you saw or experienced in your journal.

Chapter 8

Pop Culture and Fairy; Queens in a new age

Thus far we've looked at the Fairy Queens in Scottish folklore and several of the named Queens in Irish folklore. These are the Fairy Queens of history and of daily belief who people have been acknowledging for unknown amounts of time. Now as we proceed into this chapter we will be plunging into murkier waters as we enter into the realm of Fairy Queens found primarily in literature or popular culture; their historicity is often uncertain although certainly there are people today who connect to them and honour them.

Unlike previous sections this time we will not be focusing on a single being but rather this will be an overview of a variety of Fairy Queens made famous by literary works and pop culture. Often their roots before they appeared in the fiction that made them famous are unclear and while in some cases we may surmise they represented older folkloric figures we simply do not know. They are, in many ways, enigmas yet people do honour them and find powerful connections to them.

There will also be no guided meditation in this chapter, although at this point if you feel inclined to try to meet any of the Queens included here you should be able to adapt the previously included format for yourself for any one of them.

Thus far we have taken in-depth looks at Queens who appear in folklore; now we want to shift to look at the way that Queens have been portrayed by those who may or may not believe in their actual existence in fiction and literature. All of these aspects of the Fairy Queens are important to understand and add to the larger view of who and what the Fairy Queens are and how human beings relate to them.

Literary Queens: Mab, Titania, Morgen la Fey and Gloriana
Shakespeare's Fairy Queens: Mab and Titinaia

Mab

Queen Mab is a figure who first appears in Shakespeare's play 'Romeo and Juliet' written in the late 1590's. Briggs suggests that the character of Mab, although along the lines of an insect-like fairy, may have been influenced by Celtic folklore and by existing figures such as the Irish Queen Meave (Briggs, 1976). Mab is not a character in the play itself but is rather only referenced by Mercutio in a long speech he gives on the subject of dreams. He describes Queen Mab as a midwife of the fairies, as tiny as the stone in a ring, who travels at night in the half shell of a hazelnut turned into a wagon and pulled by atoms (Shakespeare, 1983). Mercutio credits Mab with bringing dreams both good and ill and also with matting the hair of horses and the hair of lazy people into elflocks[1] (Shakespeare, 1983). During the two centuries after Shakespeare wrote of her, Mab appeared in other literature as the Queen of fairies, either of all fairies or particularly of the tiny ones (Briggs, 1976). Mab appears in later literary works as well, seemingly inspired by Shakespeare's character, notably a dream sequence in Melville's 'Moby Dick' is named for her and she appears in a story by JM Barrie where she grants a wish to Peter Pan.

Rather oddly given her literary roots as a midwife, bringer of dreams, and punisher of the lazy in modern fiction she has repeatedly taken the role of villain, influencing how some people today may perceive her. In several novels she is said it be the queen of the Unseelie Court, including Jim Butcher's Dresden Files and Julie Kagawa's Iron Fey series. In the television show True Blood she is an ambiguous figure and she appears as a villain in the comic book 'Hellboy'.

Titania

Titania is a Fairy Queen who appears as an important character in Shakespeare's play 'A Midsummer Night's Dream' written in the mid 1590's. In the play she is the wife of the Fairy King Oberon and the two are fighting over a changeling child; because of the fight Titania is refusing her husband's company and so he sets one of his servants out to make her fall in love with a foolish mortal as a punishment (Shakespeare, 2004). Briggs connects Titania's name to that of the goddess Diana, suggesting that Titania was meant to be an epithet for the well-known goddess (Briggs, 1976). Diana is often associated by early modern writers with both fairies and witches so there is a certain logic to this idea. Titania's name is not widely seen elsewhere in literature although it does appear in one magical text found in the British Museum (Briggs, 1976).

Titania appears in a handful of works after Shakespeare, usually paired with Oberon or as a minor character; examples include a reference to her in Faust I and in an opera titled 'Oberon, or the Elf King's Oath'. Unlike Mab, Shakespeare's Titania did not find widespread popularity in modern culture although she does either appear, or is referenced, in some video games and literature. Perhaps her most high profile modern appearance would be as the Summer Court Queen in the Dresden Files books, although she does also appear as the Queen of the Black Court in Dana Marie Bell's 'Grey Court' series.

Arthurian Fairy Queen: Morgen la Fey[2]

Morgen le Fay is a character first found in Arthurian stories, specifically the 12th century works of Geoffrey of Monmouth, where her name was initially spelled Morgen le Fay, although it is more commonly seen today as Morgan la Fey. This is a man's name and seems to have been a confusion by the people writing the stories from whatever the original Welsh name may have been; the 12th century Morgen would have been pronounced, roughly, 'Mor-YEN' (Jones, 1997). The name Morgen is generally believed to mean 'sea born'. Interestingly morgens are a kind of Welsh water fairy roughly similar to a male mermaid (Briggs, 1976).

Geoffrey was collecting local stories from Wales and publishing them in France and while he certainly didn't invent Morgen for his Viti Merlini there is no way to know for certain how much or little he shaped the character as he preserved her; which in fairness is true for all of the Arthurian characters he wrote about. That aside, however, Geoffrey's Morgen was a priestess, one of nine sisters connected to Avalon which was a kind of Welsh Otherworld. In the 15th century Morgen would be renamed Morgan by Thomas Malory and recast as King Arthur's scheming half-sister who was set against both Arthur and his wife Guinevere. Her epithet 'la Fey' means 'the fey' and may either connect her to the fey folk or imply her role as a sorceress as both readings are viable.

Morgen is connected to healing and, perhaps, to guiding the dead or dying to Avalon/the Otherworld. She is also strongly associated with magic, enchantment and in some cases with deception. Her role even in Arthurian mythology is complex and she is viewed in some stories as a wise and ambiguous Otherworldly figure while other stories paint her as devious and dangerous.

In modern material her character is no less complex and she may be viewed by one source as a goddess, by another as a human character, and by a third as a Fairy Queen. She has been immensely popular over the years both in Arthurian re-tellings as well as in fairy-themed fiction and she may appear in these works in a variety of different guises, sometimes good and sometimes evil. There are hundreds of new Arthurian novels where Morgan can be found and it would be beyond the scope of this work to list them. Outside of Arthurian stories she is a popular Fairy Queen as well, appearing in such works as Galenorn's 'Otherworld' as a half-fairy Queen, and as an antagonist in Green's Nightside series. We see her in episodes of the television shows the Librarians and Star Gate SG-1, and in the movie The Sorcerer's Apprentice, as well as in various video games.

Spencer's Faerie Queene: Gloriana

Gloriana is a driving character of Spencer's late 16th century work, possibly representing perfection and order, as it is she who assigns the characters their quests choosing the ideal task for each one. These quests may also be telling as they represent a drive to restore order where chaos has been loosed; one knight must find and capture someone connected to a murder who is stirring strife and another must capture a dangerous beast with *"a thousand contentious tongues"* (Erickson, 1996). Gloriana is generally understood as symbolic representation of England's Queen Elizabeth and Fairy itself as seen as parallel to Elizabethan England and in the poem the two act as mirrors to each other.

Gloriana is an unusual Queen by many measures, ruling over a largely chaotic and lawless Fairy where her power seems limited to directing a handful of knights in a drive to bring perfection to chaos (Erickson, 1996). Her court is held in Fairy's only city, Cleopolis, which also serves as a goal for many characters in the poem to reach. Gloriana's Fairyland occupies a liminal place between Heaven, Hell, and mortal earth, yet is also separate from various other divine realms mentioned, making both its location and nature difficult to pin down, and is as much allegory as folklore (Erickson, 1996). Her realm is also in many ways a representation of imagination itself rather than intended to describe an actual fairy realm and no matter how much good is accomplished by her knights ultimately nothing changes.

The 1978 novel 'Gloriana, or the Unfulfilled Queen' is styled along the same lines as Spenser's work and uses allegory to retell the rule of Queen Elizabeth of England, using Gloriana as a main character, the ruler of a fictional land. Gloriana appears as the Queen of the White Court in Dana Marie Bell's 'Grey Court' series. In those books she is a difficult character who upholds an ideal of perfection that is often harmful to those she rules over. There is also an episode of the historic drama The Crown titled Gloriana.

Pop-culture Fairy Queens: The Queens in Modern Writing

Fairy Queens are often featured in modern works of fiction, although without grounding in the older source material. We have touched on a few of these as we looked at the specific literary Queens, but here we can take a better look at two examples of how these popular culture appearances play out.

Jim Butcher's Dresden Files series of novels has a complex monarchy system, wherein each of the two Courts, summer and winter, are ruled by a 'Mother', Queen, and Lady. The two 'Mothers' are never named beyond their titles. The Summer Queen is Titania; the Winter Queen is Mab. The summer Lady is initially Aurora, but she is killed during one of the books. The winter Lady is Meave. We can safely conclude from this, I think, that Butcher was drawing largely on Shakespeare for his Fairy Queens, although it is a bit of a question why he chose Mab as the Queen of the Winter Court.

In Dana Marie Bell's 'Grey Court' series Fairy has three Courts. The White Court, which is viewed as the 'good' court, is ruled by Gloriana who seeks purity and perfection among her people, rejecting anything and anyone who is perceived as less than ideal. The Grey Court is ruled by Oberon, the most powerful of the three rulers, and the Grey is a neutral court that takes in anyone; it is neither good nor evil. The Black Court is ruled by Oberon's ex-wife Titania and is the 'bad' court, filled with the monsters of Fairy. Like Butcher, Bell was looking at the older literary Queens for inspiration, blending Shakespeare and Spenser together for her world.

In Butcher's writing Titania leads what may nominally be

described as the 'good' fairies of the Summer court; in Bell's books Titania is the Queen of the dangerous fairies. Butcher assigns that role to Mab, while Bell envisions Gloriana as the Queen of the good fairies (although good in this context may be debatable). In both examples we see the author using literary queens as a springboard for their imagination to create new versions of Fairy Queens that fit the needs of their specific plots. The historic literary Queens are re-envisioned and given new lives and personalities, sometimes recreated entirely with only the name remaining the same. Modern fiction is much more accessible and relatable for many pagans today and offers a way for people to access the Fairy Queens that older literature may not. The Gloriana of modern fiction is easier to understand and feel connected to than the aloof character of Spenser's poem.

If we were to look at any of the other books or shows mentioned we would find the same thing, and this is important for those of us seeking to find the Fairy Queens in the modern world. For many people their introduction to the Queens doesn't come through folklore or literature but through fiction in some form, and this must be respected and also understood in context. Just like Marvel Comic's Thor isn't the same as the actual Norse god but can help people take those first steps to meeting him, the fictional Queens should be understood as characters rather than Otherworldly beings. But that doesn't mean those beings don't exist and can't be worked with – we must just work to unwind them from the layers of modern fictional backstory to find their true core.

If any of the literary Fairy queens appeal to you as a Queen you want to work with or connect to, I suggest reading their oldest source material. Study their journey in literature and modern fiction. Look at the way their story has changed over time and the different ways they are understood in their own contexts. What characteristics are assigned to them? Are they usually viewed as helpful or dangerous? What are they considered the

Queen of? What could their roots in folklore be? There may be no clear answers to these questions but the journey to answer them, like the quests Gloriana assigned her knights, will help you to travel further on your own spiritual path and gain a deeper understanding of that Fairy Queen.

End Notes

1   Elflocks are unexplained tangles or mats that appear in the hair of people or animals overnight, believed to be a sign of fairy anger with the person or madness. Combing them out is seen as very unlucky. In many cases they might be cut out and the person would sleep with iron to ward off any further fairy activity.

2   I am aware that in modern terms her name is often given now as Morgan la Fey however I am choosing to go with the older original spelling used by the first person to write her name down.

Chapter 9

Working with Fairy Queens

Having learned more about several of the Fairy Queens and possibly having made some initial efforts to contact them and get to know them, we will now take some time to look at further methods of connecting to the Queens. This is not in any way required, of course, and there is nothing at all wrong with choosing to study the Queens from an intellectual or folkloric perspective and not engage with them actively. This chapter, however, is aimed at people looking for more active engagement.

It's important to be clear at the beginning that just as with human relationships when we seek to engage with Fairy and its inhabitants, and especially with the Fairy Queens, there are no guaranteed outcomes. We may begin with one intention and find the situation is either more rigid or more fluid than we expected, so I always recommend trying to keep expectations to a minimum. Be clear going in what your own boundaries are and what you can and will give or do but otherwise try not to anticipate any outcomes. As with the meditations/journeys in the previous chapters creating an active relationship with these Powers may be ignored, tolerated, or warmly welcomed.

Also like human relationships while I can offer you a template here for possible ways to move forward with the Queens, or a specific Queen, how that actually manifests for you will be personal. Ultimately you must trust your own intuition and lived experience in deciding what to do and how to do it, and most importantly what risks to take and what boundaries to set and hold. No one can tell you how this will all work out for you if you choose to go forward with it and no one can promise that it will be safe or end well – or for that matter that it won't. While there are risks to working with the Queens there are also rewards which is undoubtedly why people have been drawn to seek them out over the centuries.

Sometimes a Fairy Queen will have no interest in a person, no matter how much the person tries to establish a relationship with her, while other times a person may find that a Fairy Queen – or even several – may be in or around that person's life whether or not the person wants them to be. There are historic accounts related by Emma Wilby in her book 'Cunning Folk and Familiar Spirits' of people who the Fairy Queen would visit, often in disguise at first, and later the Queen or her representative would appear to the person with an offer. I am aware of modern people who have experienced similar things, sometimes having this unknown being around them for years before they finally realize she is a Fairy Queen. Like any being with agency and independence they have their own motives and reasons for what they do and we will not always understand what those motivations are.

Levels of Work

In my opinion there are five different levels of working with the Queens. None of these is better or worse than the others, and they don't in any way reflect a progressive system; in fact one can move in any direction between these five different levels and it is possible to engage in more than one at once. Rather than being a graduated system these five simply reflect different ways in which a person's life can be focused on a Fairy Queen and how that will impact them. Each has its own specific requirements and involvements though and as with all things Fairy may carry certain obligations or risks as well.

Respecting Them – The most straightforward and easiest way for anyone to connect to a Fairy Queen is to respect them. This doesn't involve any obligations or pre-requisites and is the bare bone minimum of what a person seeking fairy amity of any sort should do anyway. Don't speak ill of them, mock them, make jokes about them, use their names irreverently[1], or say anything that implies they are powerless or weak. Treat what belongs to them well, for example if you are visiting one of their places be a good guest. Show them the basic respect you would give any deity.

Honouring Them – Slightly more involved than just showing respect, honouring a Fairy Queen could mean making occasional or regular offerings to them, acknowledging them on their special holidays, or otherwise having a regular practice relating to them. Honouring them is often as simple as leaving out some milk or a small cake in their name to recognize who and what they are on an important occasion. This level is fairly casual and means honouring the power they have and ability to influence people's lives but not asking them for much beyond friendship. Honouring a Fairy Queen is one of the more common approaches to working with them.

Dealing With Them – Probably the other most common way to work with a Queen, dealing with them can be similar to honouring them but involves more active engagement. Whereas someone honouring a Queen might leave out an offering on a holiday asking for friendship or just reciting a little poem or prayer to them, someone dealing with them would be asking them for specific things and offering specific things in exchange. This is a more directly reciprocal relationship, and I encourage people who would deal with the Fairy Queens to take a formal approach and consider it the same way they would any other transaction, where you clearly state what you are offering and what you would like to receive. This still holds true if they are the ones approaching you, although in that case they will be the ones offering and asking and you will have to decide if the terms suit.

Dedicated To Them – Dedication to any spirit, be it a deity or Fairy Queen (or King), is a serious matter and not one to take lightly. It must be acknowledged though that while such dedications can occur through advanced planning they do also happen spontaneously and are not always entirely within our control. You may find yourself in a dream or meditation dedicating yourself to a Fairy Queen even if you hadn't planned to beforehand and these experiences – even in dreams – should be treated as real.

Dedication can take various forms and can have different levels. One might dedicate as a priestess or priest of a Fairy Queen in the same way one would for a classical deity, or one might dedicate as a witch who looks to the Queen as a patron. In this case dedication means that you have chosen that particular Fairy Queen as a main focus, either temporarily or more permanently, for your spirituality. Unlike serving a Fairy Queen, which we will discuss next, being dedicated to one means that you are still primarily living your own life and doing what you need to do for your own spiritual growth but with the Fairy Queen as an important influence or guide.

Serving Them – The least common modern form of working with the Queens although perhaps the more common historic method based on what evidence we have from witch trials and ballads. To serve a Fairy Queen is pretty much what it sounds like: to be in service to that Queen and to pledge your loyalty to her. This is a very serious matter and when we see it in the historic material among people it usually involved a renunciation of the person's previous religion and spiritual oaths and a literal swearing of new oaths to the Fairy Queen. In a few cases this service is not permanent but temporary – often lasting seven years – and in those situations did not seem to involve the same level of repudiation and swearing. When one is sworn to a Fairy Queen, as opposed to dedicated to one, priorities shift into focusing on that Queen in a different and deeper way and generally to having a stronger allegiance to Fairy itself over the human world.

Serving a Fairy Queen inherently involves giving up a

degree of autonomy and is something that needs to be seriously considered before being agreed to.

For many people simply respecting the Fairy Queens will be enough, perhaps combined with studying them. For others there may be some shifting back and forth between honouring them and dealing with them, particularly for people who choose to incorporate fairies more generally into their spirituality or who walk the line between seeing some of these beings as Fairy Queens and/or Goddesses. Whatever type of focus you find yourself drawn to you should try to enter into it consciously and with an awareness of what you are doing.

Negotiating

Negotiation is one of the main things underpinning most of our relationships with the Otherworld. Even things that seem like ultimatums are often negotiable and as we seek to learn to work with the Queens it's important to finely hone our negotiating skills. They will expect that anything promised will be done or given and that agreements will be kept so you should never agree to anything you aren't comfortable with. This will also come into play as we move between or seek the different levels I just discussed, because both we and they can negotiate where we want to be at (or where they would like us at) and what our terms are.

It may seem odd to some people to think of negotiating with higher powers or spirits, but this really is an important aspect of dealing with these beings. Sometimes we may want their help with something and we need to be very clear on what we are willing to give for that help; other times they may come to us, in dreams, visions, or meditations, and offer specific things including teaching or protection but again we need to be careful to consider the cost. Nothing is free.

Sacred Space and Pilgrimage

One important way to include the Fairy Queens in your life, in any sense, is through physical space. Physical sacred spaces, whether they are a picture on a wall, a small indoor shrine, or a large outdoor location, give us a tangible anchor to focus on as well as care for. Physical spaces may also be public places that have historically or in stories been associated with a Fairy Queen and have strong energetic ties to that being; Loch Gur's connection to Áine for example or Nicnevin's association with Ben Nevis. The point of having or visiting these physical spaces is that they can help you anchor yourself and your spiritual connection to these Powers that are themselves so often strongly connected to specific locations. They give you a touchstone, rather literally, to focus your connection on.

In the previous sections we have briefly looked at setting up small altars or shrines to each Queen, and if you choose to move forward in connection to one or more you can make that space more permanent. You may also look at expanding this idea into a larger space or modifying it into something more permanent. When it comes to a more elaborate shrine your own imagination and your available space are your only limits, and you should trust your instinct for what will work best and makes the most sense in the space. I would suggest if you are going to look at working with several Fairy Queens to very carefully feel out how they are together before combining shrine spaces and avoid putting two Queens together who have known issues with each other in folklore or mythology (Cliodhna and Aoibheall for example).

You may also consider if possible visiting the real-world locations associated with the Fairy Queen(s) who interests you. This sort of pilgrimage to a sacred site can often have deep and powerful impacts that we don't foresee until we are there and can be transformative for our spirituality. Of course physical travel is not always an option for many reasons[2] and in that case you can meditate on the location or consider getting pictures of the place to act as that same kind of focus.

If Things Go Wrong

Most of what we've discussed here is based on the idea of things going well or a worst case scenario of you being ignored. Realistically though that isn't really the worst thing that might happen[3] so before we finish this chapter I do want to touch on suggestions of how to handle things if they go truly badly. Hopefully you can avoid this by remembering what was discussed at the beginning of the book about etiquette and good manners, but even with the best intentions sometimes we end up giving offense without meaning to. Let's assume here that you have somehow managed to do that and are dealing with the consequences which can range from unpleasant to severe.

What do you do?

The first step, in any case of offending the Gentry, is to apologize profusely and sincerely. I find it helps to explain why the faux pas happened and make it clear that you will try to avoid doing the same thing again. Another good step towards and effective apology is to offer compensation or give them something you know they like; whatever you might normally consider a suitable offering this should be better. It also helps to make sure your actions are in line with your words; if you are saying you are sorry you should be acting like you are sorry. If any physical damage is involved or if a physical item is involved that should also be dealt with if possible.

Justice in Fairy in my experience is restorative justice where an emphasis is placed on the offender fixing whatever harm was caused and restoring order. This is not always as easily said as done when what was harmed was someone's honour or feelings but it gives you an idea of what you should be trying to do anyway. It may take time and effort, but if you work at it you should be able to effectively apologize for any social misstep you make that upsets one of the Queens.

Deepening Your Work

Once you've established some of the basics discussed here all that's left is to move forward organically. Learn from them, if you can, and establish your own rhythm and balance for how they fit into your life and spirituality. Perhaps you will find that the Queens, or one Queen in particular, become cornerstones of your spirituality or perhaps they will be Powers you respect and only occasionally engage with. There's no right or wrong for how you move forward from here, or even any requirement that you must do so.

End Notes

1   For example some pagans or modern authors make up clever expressions to use in place of the name of the Christian God in cursing, like 'By Odin's Ravens' or the more colourful 'Dagda's Balls'. It's understandable and certain deities seem to have a sense of humour about this sort of thing, which is why I used the Dagda as an example. But in my own experience the Fairy Queens I have named in this book aren't ones I'd recommend accidently invoking by pairing their name with a body part or bodily function.

2   Travel is a privilege and should be appreciated as such, and there are an array of reasons that might prohibit anyone from travelling to a location, including physical health, mobility, or finances. It should also be kept in mind that not all sacred sites associated with Fairy Queens are on public property or have public access, and if you are able to travel you still need to be certain the location is legally accessible.

3   There are numerous accounts in folklore and anecdotal material of people who offend the Fair Folk suffering consequences ranging from physical abuse including bruising and pinching, illness (which in some cases lasted for years), maiming, madness or other mental health issues, or a loss of luck and wealth.

Conclusion

The Fairy Queens are fascinating personages, as alive and powerful today as they have ever been, yet perhaps even more mysterious and hard to understand. Goddesses whose worship shifted into something else over time they have never truly left this world. They can be found still in folklore and poetry and they have seen a resurgence in popularity in novels and even on television, playing the villain as often as not in novels like the Dresden Files and on shows like The Magicians. A modern pagan seeking to understand or even substantially connect to a Fairy Queen finds a maze to navigate between Shakespeare's Queen Mab and Harry Dresden's version of the same name, while someone seeking Clíodhna may be equally lost in a sea of campy banshee art and obscure antiquarian folklore texts. Finding the truth becomes an exercise in both research and experiential gnosis.

In these pages you have learned the basics of fairy etiquette, how to meet and work with your fairy Guide, how to navigate Fairy, and you have met many of the Fairy Queens. Whether or not any of them spoke to you – literally or figuratively – learning more about them has its own value and in learning more about them you have gained insight into Fairy itself. What you choose to do with this knowledge now is up to you.

The Bibliography that follows can offer you potential resources to look further into each of the Queens if you'd like. You can find the Queens who used to be Goddesses in mythology by finding the myths they were recorded in and also trace their tales in folklore. I'd also suggest seeking out storytellers within the living cultures and also trying to experience the literary Queens directly, perhaps by reading the books they appear in or seeing their plays preformed. The ballad material can be read as well as listened to in song form. The Fairy Queens can be engaged with in many ways and the more methods you seek the deeper you will find your understanding of them growing, because as much as we need to seek them out in their living active selves we also need to know them as history has understood them and as our own ancestors would have viewed them. Like the world they rule over they are an inherent contradiction: timeless and also ever evolving, unchanging and yet never the same.

However you seek them from here know that no one source or person or experience will ever hold the entire truth of who they are. They are larger than anyone can truly conceive of. They are generous as much as they are dangerous and they are kind as often as they are cruel. They are the endless contradiction of life that dictates that all things born must die but that in death new life will be fed. They are the poetry of a swordfight. And the comfort of honey on your lips. All of these things and more, because words will never do them justice.

Ultimately this book, like any book, can only ever be a single stepping stone for you.

May it lead you where you need to be.

Bibliography

Acland, A., (1997) Tam Lin Child Ballad 39A retrieved from tam-lin.org

Acland, A., (2018) Tam Lin 39 G retrieved from tam-lin.org

Acland, A., (1997) Thomas the Rhymer retrieved from tam-lin. org

Acland, A., (2001) The Ballad of Alison Gross retrieved from tam-lin.org

An Buachaill Caol Dubh - folk song, various versions

Barry, G., (1867) A History of the Orkney Islands

Briggs, K., (1976) A Dictionary of Fairies

Brosius, M., (2007). The Court and Court Society in Ancient Monarchies

Buchan, D., (1991) 'Ballads of Otherworld Beings', The Good People

C&MH (2014) Castle Life: Officers and Servants in a Medieval Castle retrieved from http://www.castlesandmanorhouses. com/life_02_officers.htm

Campbell, J., (1900) The Gaelic Otherworld

Carraig Cliona (2018) Duchais.ie archive Retrieved from https:// www.duchas.ie/en/cbes/4921783/4906795/5178148?Chapter ID=4921783

Carson, C., (2006) The Midnight Court

Child, J., (1882) The English and Scottish Popular Ballads vol 1

Croker, T. (1834). Fairy Legends and Traditions of the South of Ireland

Cromek (1810) Remains of Nithsdale and Galloway Song

Cussen, M., (1929) Cork Weekly Examiner, October 8th Issue

Dinneen, P., (1900) Dánta Aodhagháin Uí Rathaille

DSL (2017) NicNevin, Dictionary of the Scots Language

Duchais.ie (2018) Knockshegowna Retrieved from https://www. duchas.ie/en/src?q=knockshegowna

Ellis, P., (1987). A Dictionary of Irish Mythology

Erickson, W., (1996) Mapping the Faerie Queene: Quest Structure and the World of the Poem

Heirarchy Structure (2018) The Royal Court retrieved from https://www.hierarchystructure.com/royal-court-hierarchy/

Henderson, L., and Cowan, E., (2007) Scottish Fairy Belief

Jones, H., (1997) Concerning the Names Morgan, Morgana, Morgaine, Muirghein, Morrigan and the Like. Retrieved from https://medievalscotland.org/problem/names/morgan.shtml

Joyce, P., (1869) Irish Names of Places

Lane, J., and Clifford, B., (1993) A North Cork Anthology

Logainm.ie (2018) Knockshigowna https://www.logainm.ie/ga/45803

Marshall, R., (2013). Clare Folk tales

MacKillop, J., (1998) A Dictionary of Celtic Mythology

McNeill, F., (1962) Festival of Lughnasa

Merriman, B., (2006) The Midnight Court - translated by Ciaran Carson

Miller, J., (2004). Magic and Witchcraft in Scotland.

Monaghan, P., (2004). The Encyclopedia of Celtic Mythology and Folklore

Morgan la Fay (2018) The Camelot Project; University of Rochester. Retrieved from http://www.kingarthursknights.com/others/morganlefay.asp

Pattie, T., (2011) Medieval People, Titles, Trades, and Classes retrieved from http://go.vsb.bc.ca/schools/templeton/departments/socialstudies/MsRamsey/Documents/Medieval%20People.pdf

O hOgain, D., (2006) Lore of Ireland

O'Kearny, N., (1855) Feis Tighe Chonain Chinn-Shleibhe, Or, The Festivities at the House of Conan of Ceann-Sleibhe, in the County of Clare

Ryan, D., (2016) Kncoksheegowna http://thetipperaryantiquarian.blogspot.com/2016/07/knocksheegowna.html

Scott, W., (1802). Minstrelsy of the Scottish Borders

--- (1820). The Abbott

--- (1831) Letters on Demonologie and Witchcraft

Shakespeare, W., (1983) Romeo and Juliet

--- (2004) A Midsummer Night's Dream

Smyth, D., (1988) Irish Mythology

Thoms, W., (1884) The Book of the Court: Exhibiting the History, Duties, and Privileges of the English Nobility and Gentry

Westropp, T., (1910). Folklore of Clare

Wilby, E., (2005) Cunning Folk and Familiar Spirits

MOON

BOOKS

PAGANISM & SHAMANISM

What is Paganism? A religion, a spirituality, an alternative
belief system, nature worship? You can find support for all these
definitions (and many more) in dictionaries, encyclopaedias, and
text books of religion, but subscribe to any one and the truth will
evade you. Above all Paganism is a creative pursuit, an encounter
with reality, an exploration of meaning and an expression of the
soul. Druids, Heathens, Wiccans and others, all contribute their
insights and literary riches to the Pagan tradition. Moon Books
invites you to begin or to deepen your own encounter, right here,
right now.
If you have enjoyed this book, why not tell other readers by
posting a review on your preferred book site.

Recent bestsellers from Moon Books are:

Journey to the Dark Goddess
How to Return to Your Soul
Jane Meredith
Discover the powerful secrets of the Dark Goddess and transform your depression, grief and pain into healing and integration.
Paperback: 978-1-84694-677-6 ebook: 978-1-78099-223-5

Shamanic Reiki
Expanded Ways of Working with Universal Life Force Energy
Llyn Roberts, Robert Levy
Shamanism and Reiki are each powerful ways of healing; together, their power multiplies. *Shamanic Reiki* introduces techniques to help healers and Reiki practitioners tap ancient healing wisdom.
Paperback: 978-1-84694-037-8 ebook: 978-1-84694-650-9

Pagan Portals – The Awen Alone
Walking the Path of the Solitary Druid
Joanna van der Hoeven
An introductory guide for the solitary Druid, *The Awen Alone* will accompany you as you explore, and seek out your own place within the natural world.
Paperback: 978-1-78279-547-6 ebook: 978-1-78279-546-9

A Kitchen Witch's World of Magical Herbs & Plants
Rachel Patterson
A journey into the magical world of herbs and plants, filled with magical uses, folklore, history and practical magic. By popular writer, blogger and kitchen witch, Tansy Firedragon.
Paperback: 978-1-78279-621-3 ebook: 978-1-78279-620-6

Medicine for the Soul
The Complete Book of Shamanic Healing
Ross Heaven
All you will ever need to know about shamanic healing and how to
become your own shaman...
Paperback: 978-1-78099-419-2 ebook: 978-1-78099-420-8

Shaman Pathways – The Druid Shaman
Exploring the Celtic Otherworld
Danu Forest
A practical guide to Celtic shamanism with exercises and
techniques as well as traditional lore for exploring the Celtic
Otherworld.
Paperback: 978-1-78099-615-8 ebook: 978-1-78099-616-5

Traditional Witchcraft for the Woods and Forests
A Witch's Guide to the Woodland with Guided Meditations and
Pathworking
Mélusine Draco
A Witch's guide to walking alone in the woods, with guided
meditations and pathworking.
Paperback: 978-1-84694-803-9 ebook: 978-1-84694-804-6

Wild Earth, Wild Soul
A Manual for an Ecstatic Culture
Bill Pfeiffer
Imagine a nature-based culture so alive and so connected,
spreading like wildfire. This book is the first flame...
Paperback: 978-1-78099-187-0 ebook: 978-1-78099-188-7

Naming the Goddess
Trevor Greenfield
Naming the Goddess is written by over eighty adherents and scholars of Goddess and Goddess Spirituality.
Paperback: 978-1-78279-476-9 ebook: 978-1-78279-475-2

Shapeshifting into Higher Consciousness
Heal and Transform Yourself and Our World with Ancient Shamanic and Modern Methods
Llyn Roberts
Ancient and modern methods that you can use every day to transform yourself and make a positive difference in the world.
Paperback: 978-1-84694-843-5 ebook: 978-1-84694-844-2

Readers of ebooks can buy or view any of these bestsellers by clicking on the live link in the title. Most titles are published in paperback and as an ebook. Paperbacks are available in traditional bookshops. Both print and ebook formats are available online.

Find more titles and sign up to our readers' newsletter at
http://www.johnhuntpublishing.com/paganism
Follow us on Facebook at https://www.facebook.com/MoonBooks
and Twitter at https://twitter.com/MoonBooksJHP